Das energieeffiziente Frankfurt

The energy-efficient Frankfurt

Reiseführer Travel-Guide

Impressum:
Herausgeber: Weststadt Verlag, Energiereferat der Stadt Frankfurt am Main, Smart Skript
Idee, Projektmanagement, Autorin: Bettina Gehbauer-Schumacher, Smart Skript
Übersetzung: Meeta Kukadia-Just
Gestaltung und Satz: Lindenmayer + Lehning, Darmstadt
Druck und Bindung: Ph. Reinheimer GmbH, Darmstadt

© 2013 Weststadt Verlag
ISBN 978-3-940179-15-9

Inhalt

Grußwort	4
Klimaschutz in Frankfurt am Main	6
Historie	10

Routen/Tours

1 ǀ Gallus	14
2 ǀ Sachsenhausen – Mainufer – Westhafen	22
3 ǀ Westend Süd – Europaviertel – Westend Nord	38
4 ǀ Westend Süd – Innenstadt – Nordend	66
5 ǀ City – Innenstadt und Altstadt	84
6 ǀ Exkursionen	104

Service	134
Glossar	140
Unterstützer und Sponsoren	145
Fotoverzeichnis, Karten und Pläne	158
Quellenverzeichnis	159
Index	160

Grußwort

Ich freue mich über Ihr Interesse an einer Stadtbesichtigung der besonderen Art. Denn neben Römer, Museumsufer und Skyline hat Frankfurt zahlreiche Klimaschutz-Highlights zu bieten. Wussten Sie, dass der Commerzbank-Tower nicht nur das höchste Bürogebäude Deutschlands, sondern auch ein Vorreiter bei energiesparender Gebäudetechnik ist? Oder dass Frankfurt die Hauptstadt der Passivhäuser ist – nirgends leben mehr Menschen in diesen besonders energiesparenden Wohnungen. Ich lade Sie ein, sich mit diesem Stadtführer auf Entdeckungstour zu begeben und Frankfurts ‚grüne' Gebäude und Energieanlagen zu erkunden.

Ihre Rosemarie Heilig
Dezernentin für Umwelt und Gesundheit
Stadt Frankfurt am Main

Welcome

I am pleased that you have shown an interest in this special kind of a sightseeing tour. Frankfurt provides important sights – the 'Römer', the museums' embankment and the skyline – and numerous climate protection highlights.

Did you know that the Commerzbank Tower is not only the tallest office building in Germany, but also a pioneer in energy-saving building technology, or that the City of Frankfurt is the capital of Passive Houses: nowhere do more people live in this type of highly energy-efficient home? I invite you with this guide to go on a discovery tour and explore Frankfurt's 'green' buildings and energy installations.

Yours, Rosemarie Heilig
Head of Department for Health and Environment
City of Frankfurt

Vorwort

Klimaschutz in Frankfurt am Main

Bereits im Jahr 1990 hatte die Stadt Frankfurt am Main ihre Verpflichtung für den Klimaschutz dokumentiert, indem sie das Klima-Bündnis mitgründete und ihm zugleich beitrat. Inzwischen haben sich 1.600 Städte, Gemeinden und Landkreise in 20 europäischen Ländern dazu bekannt, ihren CO_2-Ausstoß alle fünf Jahre um 10% zu verringern.

Die Stadt hat sich seither verpflichtet, systematisch Klimaschutz zu betreiben, ihn bei städtischen Entscheidungen zu berücksichtigen, Bürger und Firmen zu beteiligen und regelmäßig über die Fortschritte zu berichten. Nach 20 Jahren Arbeit gehört Frankfurt nicht nur in Deutschland, sondern in ganz Europa zur Spitzenliga im Bereich Klimaschutz.

Mit Kraft-Wärme-Kopplung Energie vor Ort effizient nutzen

Mit Kraft-Wärme-Kopplung werden mehr als 90% der Energie als Strom- und Wärme genutzt. In Großkraftwerken werden dagegen 40–60% der Energie verschwendet. Drei große Heizkraftwerke und 10 dezentrale Wärmenetze, über 250 dezentrale Kraft-Wärme-Kopplungs-Anlagen, 2 Biogas- und eine holzbefeuerte Anlage im Megawatt-Bereich liefern mehr als 50% der Elektrizität in Frankfurt mit hoher Effizienz. Damit werden mehr als 1 Mio. t CO_2 pro Jahr eingespart.

Frankfurt – Hauptstadt der Passivhäuser

Frankfurt am Main ist Spitzenreiter beim Bau von Passivhäusern. Städtische Gebäude und Gebäude der ABG Frankfurt Holding Wohnungsbau- und Beteiligungsgesellschaft mbH werden nur noch im Passivhausstandard errichtet. Nach einem Beschluss der Stadtverordneten muss auch beim Kauf eines städtischen Grundstückes das neue Gebäude den Passivhausstandard erfüllen. Bislang wurden von der Stadt Frankfurt 2 Feuerwachen, 5 Jugendhäuser, 10 Kindertagesstätten, 10 Schulen bzw. Schulerweiterungen, 12 Schulmensen, 5 Sportfunktionsgebäude und 6 Turnhallen als Passivhäuser fertiggestellt. Weitere 50 Projekte befinden sich in Planung oder im Bau.

Frankfurts ‚grüne' Skyline

Auch Frankfurts Skyline wird immer ‚grüner'. Nach einer Auswertung des Maklerunternehmens Jones Lang LaSalle haben in Frankfurt inzwischen 50 Gebäude ein Nachhaltigkeitszertifikat oder sind für eine Zertifizierung angemeldet. Damit hat Frankfurt bundesweit den Spitzenplatz bei der Anzahl zertifizierter ‚grüner' Gebäude erobert.

Climate protection in Frankfurt

As early as 1990, the city of Frankfurt committed itself to climate protection by co-founding and then joining the Climate Alliance. Since then 1,600 cities, communities and counties in 20 European countries have pledged to reduce their CO_2 emissions by 10% every five years.

Climate protection is taken into consideration in all municipal decisions by the city and it has pledged to involve citizens and businesses and to report regularly on progress made. After 20 years of working in this direction, Frankfurt belongs, not only in Germany but throughout Europe, to the top league of climate protectors.

Local energy used efficiently by utilizing combined heat and power

With combined heat and power more than 90% of the energy can be used as heat and electricity. In contrast, in large power plants, 40–60% of the energy is wasted. Three major thermal power stations and 10 local heat networks, over 250 combined heat and power plants, two biogas-plants and a wood-fired plant in the megawatt range provide more than 50% of electricity in Frankfurt with high efficiency. Thus, more than 1 million tons of CO_2 are saved per year.

Frankfurt – Capital of Passive Houses

The City of Frankfurt is the leader in the construction of Passive Houses. Municipal buildings and buildings of the ABG Frankfurt Holding Wohnungsbau- und Beteiligungsgesellschaft mbH will only be built according to Passive House standards. Following a decision of the city council any new building must meet the Passive House standard when an urban plot is purchased.

So far the city of Frankfurt has built 2 fire stations, 5 youth centres, 10 kindergartens, 10 schools or school extensions, 12 school canteens and 11 gymnasiums all according to Passive House standards. Another 50 projects are currently in planning or under construction.

Frankfurt's 'green' Skyline

Frankfurt's skyline is getting 'greener' as time goes by. After an evaluation of the brokerage firm Jones Lang LaSalle, 50 buildings in Frankfurt have a sustainability certificate already or are currently undergoing a certification. Thus, Frankfurt has captured the top spot nationwide for the number of certified 'green' buildings.

Green Building Award
Mit dem Green Building Award würdigen die Städte Frankfurt und Darmstadt sowie der Regionalverband FrankfurtRheinMain Architekten und Bauherren für ihren Beitrag zu Baukultur und Klimaschutz. Die Preisträger – ob Wohnhaus, Schule oder Bürogebäude – zeigen, wie schön und nutzerfreundlich nachhaltige Architektur sein kann. Drei Eigenschaften zeichnen die Preisträger von Green Building FrankfurtRheinMain aus: Sie sind innovativ, gestalterisch hochwertig und nachhaltig.

Klimaschutzstadtplan Frankfurt
Viele Klimaschutzprojekte – ob Passivhaus, Solaranlage oder Blockheizkraftwerk – sind im Klimaschutzstadtplan Frankfurt verzeichnet. Unter www.klimaschutzstadtplan-frankfurt.de bekommt man einen Überblick sowie Detailinformationen zu vielen Anlagen und Gebäuden.

Masterplan 100% Klimaschutz für Frankfurt
Mit dem ‚Masterplan 100% Klimaschutz' will die Stadt Frankfurt ihr Klimaschutzkonzept weiterentwickeln und herausfinden, wie eine vollständige Versorgung mit erneuerbaren Energien bis zum Jahr 2050 möglich sein kann. Mehr als 70% der Energie wird in Städten verbraucht, weshalb bei der Energiewende den Städten eine besondere Rolle zukommt. Gut die Hälfte des heutigen Strom- und Wärmebedarfs kann durch Energieeffizienz eingespart werden. Die andere Hälfte könnte mit erneuerbaren Energien aus dem Stadtgebiet und der Region gedeckt werden.
Energieeinsparung ist deshalb auch Kern des Masterplans 100% Klimaschutz. Die größten Potenziale liegen hier bei den Gebäuden. Bei den meisten Häusern kann durch Sanierung der Energiebedarf um mehr als 50% reduziert werden.
Hauptziel wird es auch in Zukunft sein, Gebäude zu bauen, die so wenig Energie verbrauchen wie möglich. Der verbleibende geringe Energiebedarf sollte dann effizient mit erneuerbaren Energien gedeckt werden, denn auch erneuerbare Energien benötigen Fläche, kosten Geld und verbrauchen Umweltressourcen. Das Passivhaus ist deshalb eine gute Grundlage für innovative Häuser, die mehr Energie erzeugen als sie verbrauchen.
Zukünftig wird vor allem die energetische Modernisierung ganzer Stadtteile und Wohnviertel im Fokus stehen. Hier kann Frankfurt seine Erfahrungen im Passivhausbau, bei Wärmenetzen mit Kraft-Wärme-Kopplung und Solarenergie nutzen. Die Umgestaltung einer gesamten Stadt hin zu 100% erneuerbare Energie ist eine große Herausforderung – doch Frankfurt will den Weg zur ‚Green City' gehen.

Green Building Award

The cities of Frankfurt and Darmstadt as well as the Regional Association FrankfurtRheinMain are recognising architects and builders with the Green Building Award for their contributions to building culture and climate protection. The award winners – whether residential, school or office building – show how beautiful and user-friendly sustainable architecture can be. Three main features distinguish the winners of Green Building FrankfurtRheinMain: they are innovative, have a high quality of design and are sustainable. Twelve buildings in Frankfurt and adjoining area have already received the award.

The City of Frankfurt's climate protection plan

Many climate protection projects – whether Passive House, solar panel systems or CHP plants – are listed in the city's climate protection plan under www.klimaschutzstadtplan-frankfurt.de. An overview as well as detailed information on many plants and buildings in Frankfurt is given.

Master Plan for 100% Climate Protection in Frankfurt

With the 'Master Plan 100% Climate Protection', the city of Frankfurt wants to develop its climate protection concept and find out, how a complete power supply with renewable energy is possible by 2050.

More than 70% of the energy is consumed in cities, which is why they have a significant role during the energy revolution. Half of today's electricity and heat requirements can be saved through energy efficiency. The other half could be covered by renewable energy from the urban area and the region.

Therefore, energy saving is the core of the Master Plan 100% Climate Protection. The greatest potential lies in the buildings. Through renovation, the energy demand in most houses can be reduced by more than 50%.

In the future, the main goal will be to build buildings that consume as little energy as possible. The remaining low energy requirements should be covered with renewable energy, as even renewable energy needs space, costs money and consumes natural resources. Therefore, Passive Houses are a good basis for innovative buildings that generate more energy than they consume.

Especially in the future the energy modernisation of entire neighbourhoods and residential areas will be in focus.

Frankfurt can well utilize its experience in Passive House construction and heating networks with combined heat and power and solar energy. The transformation of an entire city to 100% renewable energy is a major challenge – but Frankfurt wants to go in this direction to become a 'Green City'.

Historie

Historischer Überblick

Begünstigt durch die Lage am Fluss ist Frankfurt seit je her ein wichtiges urbanes Zentrum für Handel, Gewerbe und Finanzwesen. Hier wurden Könige gewählt und Kaiser gekrönt – später nahm die deutsche Demokratie von dort ihren Anfang. Bürgerengagement, Kunst und Kultur werden groß geschrieben. Für Spannung sorgt der überall zu spürende Mix aus Tradition und Moderne. Ihre einzigartige Skyline gibt der größten Stadt des Landes Hessen auch ihren Spitznamen ‚Mainhattan'.

22. Februar 794 | Erste urkundliche Erwähnung als ‚Franconofurd' unter Karl dem Großen

852 | Einweihung der Pfalzkapelle (St. Salvator, später Kaiserdom St. Bartholomäus). Frankfurt ist einer der Hauptsitze des ostfränkischen Reichs.

1222 | Erste urkundliche Erwähnung der Alten Brücke. Sie wird später mehrmals zerstört und wieder aufgebaut.

1240 | Kaiser Friedrich II. gewährt der Stadt das Messeprivileg. Die jährliche Herbstmesse und die Frühjahrsmesse ab 1330 machen Frankfurt zum Zentrum des europäischen Fernhandels.

1356 bis 1806 | Frankfurt ist ständige Stätte für die deutsche Königswahl, ab 1562 zudem Krönungsstadt der Kaiser.

1372 | Reichsstadt mit eigener Finanzhoheit, Gerichtsbarkeit und Verwaltung

1405 | Aus den Privathäusern ‚Römer' und ‚Goldener Schwan' entsteht das neue Rathaus.

Um 1480 | Die Buchmesse wird fester Bestandteil der Frankfurter Messe auf dem Römerberg.

28. August 1749 | Geburt von Johann Wolfgang Goethe. Sein Geburtshaus am Großen Hirschgraben kann besichtigt werden.

1806 | Auflösung des Alten Reichs, Frankfurt verliert den Status einer selbstständigen Reichsstadt. Unter Fürstprimas Karl Theodor von Dalberg wird es 1810 bis 1813 Großherzogtum.

1815 | Auf Beschluss des Wiener Kongresses tritt der Deutsche Bund an die Stelle des Heiligen Römischen Reichs Deutscher Nation. Sein oberstes Organ, der Bundestag, sitzt im Palais Thurn und Taxis in der freien Stadt Frankfurt.

1820 | Handel der ersten Aktie an der Frankfurter Börse, die 1879 ihr neues Domizil am Börsenplatz bezieht.

1848 | Märzrevolution. Die am 18. Mai 1848 einberufene Nationalversammlung, das erste frei gewählte gesamtdeutsche Parlament, tagt in der Paulskirche.

History

Historical Overview

Benefiting from its location beside the river, Frankfurt has always been an important urban centre for trade, commerce and finance. This is the city where kings were elected and emperors were crowned – and is also the birthplace of German democracy. Civil engagement, arts and culture are of great importance. The mix of traditional and modern ensures a buzzing atmosphere which can be felt everywhere. The unique skyline gives Frankfurt the nickname 'Mainhattan'.

22nd February 794 | First documented evidence of Frankfurt as 'Franconofurd' under Charlemagne

852 | Inauguration of the Pfalzkapelle (St. Salvatore, later St. Bartholomew's Cathedral). Frankfurt is one of the headquarters of the East-Frankonian kingdom.

1222 | First documented reference of the Alte Brücke, which was later destroyed and rebuilt several times.

1240 | Emperor Friedrich II granted the city the right to hold fairs. The annual autumn and spring fairs as of 1330 make Frankfurt the centre of European long-distance trading.

1356 to 1806 | Frankfurt is the permanent location for the German royal elections, as of 1562 it also is the city for Emperor Coronations.

1372 | Imperial city with its own financial sovereignty, jurisdiction and administration

1405 | The private houses, 'Römer' and 'Goldener Schwan' are combined to form the new Town Hall.

Around 1480 | The book fair is an inherent part of the Frankfurter Messe on Römerberg.

28th August 1749 | Birth of Johann Wolfgang Goethe. The birthplace at am Großen Hirschengraben can be visited.

1806 | Disbandment of the Old Kingdom, Frankfurt loses its status as an independent imperial city. Under Prince Primate Karl Theodor von Dalberg it is a Grand Duchy from 1810 to 1813.

1815 | The Congress of Vienna decides that the German Confederation takes the place of the Holy Roman Empire. Its governing body is the parliament which is located at the Palace Thurn und Taxis in the free city of Frankfurt.

1820 | Market trading of the first share on Frankfurt's stock exchange, which moves into its new home at Börsenplatz in 1879.

1848 | March Revolution. On 18th May, 1848 the National Assembly, the first freely elected all-German parliament, convenes in the Paulskirche.

Historie

1866 | Auflösung des Deutschen Bundes. Frankfurt wird von Preußen annektiert und verliert seine Unabhängigkeit: Es wird dem Regierungsbezirk Wiesbaden zugeordnet.

1914 | Aus Bürgerstiftungen entsteht die Universität, die 1932 den Namen Johann Wolfgang Goethe-Universität erhält.

1925 bis 1930 | Stadtbaurat Ernst May errichtet mit zahlreichen Wohnsiedlungen das ‚Neue Frankfurt'.

1943/44 | Die Innen- und Altstadt werden im Krieg fast vollständig zerstört, so dass das bis 1944 nahezu geschlossene mittelalterliche Stadtbild verloren geht. Der Wiederaufbau in den 1950er Jahren orientiert sich nicht an den alten Strukturen.

1945 | Als erste deutsche Tageszeitung nach dem Krieg erscheint ab August die Frankfurter Rundschau. 1949 folgt die erste Ausgabe der Frankfurter Allgemeinen Zeitung.

1949 | Nach Kriegsende war Frankfurt Verwaltungssitz der Trizone. Mit der Gründung der Bundesrepublik Deutschland wird Bonn Bundeshauptstadt.

1953 | 1. Hochhausplan zur Reglementierung des Hochhausbaus. In der Folge wurden mehrere Konzepte erarbeitet, wie der Hochhausentwicklungsplan 1998 und seine Fortschreibung 2008. Prinzip ist, Hochhäuser möglichst in Gruppen anzuordnen.

1957 | Die Deutsche Bundesbank nimmt ihre Geschäfte am 1. August in Frankfurt auf.

1984 | Auftakt zum Ausbau des Museumsufers mit der Eröffnung des Film- und des Deutschen Architekturmuseums

1994 | Der Frankfurter Grüngürtel, ein ringförmig um den Stadtkern gelagertes Landschaftsschutzgebiet, wird ausgewiesen.

1997 | Fertigstellung des Commerzbank-Turms: Das erste ‚Green Building' der Welt und mit rund 259 m seinerzeit das höchste Gebäude Europas

1998 | Die Europäische Zentralbank hat ihren Sitz in Frankfurt.

2006 | Frankfurt ist Austragungsort der FIFA WM 2006 und richtet 2011 bei den 6. Fußball-Weltmeisterschaften der Frauen das Finale aus.

2010 | Abriss des Technischen Rathauses zwischen Dom und Römerberg, um die historische Altstadt zu rekonstruieren. Frankfurt wird ‚Klimaschutzkommune 2010'.

2012 | Finalist beim Wettbewerb um die Europäische Grüne Hauptstadt 2014

History

1866 | Disbandment of the German Confederation. Frankfurt is annexed by Prussia and loses its independence: it is assigned to the district of Wiesbaden.

1914 | Out of community foundations the university comes into being, which is to be named Johann Wolfgang Goethe University in 1932.

1925–1930 | The head of the municipal planning office Ernst May built the 'New Frankfurt' with numerous housing developments.

1943/44 | The historic and the city centre are almost completely destroyed during the war, thus, by 1944 the medieval cityscape is completely lost. The reconstruction in the 1950s is not based on the old structures.

1945 | In August, the first German daily newspaper after the war, the Frankfurter Rundschau is published. 1949 the first edition of the Frankfurter Allgemeine Zeitung follows.

1949 | After the war the headquarters of the Trizone was Frankfurt. With the foundation of the Federal Republic of Germany, Bonn is elected federal capital.

1953 | First high-rise plan for the regimentation of high-rise construction. Subsequently, several concepts have been developed, such as the high-rise development plan of 1998 and its update from 2008. Where possible, high-rises should be arranged in groups.

1957 | The Deutsche Bundesbank starts operating in Frankfurt on 1 August.

1984 | Prelude to the expansion of the Museums embankment are the openings of the Film museum and the German Architecture museum.

1994 | Frankfurt's green belt, a ring-type area located around the city centre, is declared as a conservation area.

1997 | Completion of the Commerzbank tower. At that time the first 'Green Building' in the world and the tallest building in Europe, with around 259m.

1998 | The European Central Bank has a registered office in Frankfurt.

2006 | Frankfurt hosts the FIFA World Cup of 2006 and, in 2011, hosts the final of the 6th Women's Football World Cup.

2010 | Demolition of the technical Town Hall between the cathedral and the Römerberg in order to reconstruct the historical city centre. Frankfurt is appointed 'Climate Protection Community 2010'.

2012 | Finalist in the European Green Capital Award 2014

1 | Gallus

Gallus:

Früheres Galgenfeld westlich der mittelalterlichen Stadtgrenze Frankfurts, das fast fünf Jahrhunderte als Hinrichtungsstätte diente. Der Name leitet sich von der Galgenwarte (Galluswarte) her, einem der vier mittelalterlichen Warttürme der Stadt. Erst ab Ende des 18. Jahrhunderts wird der Name auf den Heiligen Gallus bezogen.

Ein *Passivhaus* erfüllt einen bestimmten Energiestandard, ist sehr gut wärmegedämmt und benötigt keine Heizungsanlage im herkömmlichen Sinn. Der Heizenergiebedarf wird überwiegend durch Sonneneinstrahlung und die Abwärme von Personen und technischen Geräten gedeckt.

Route Gallus

Mit dem Bau des Hauptbahnhofs 1888 entwickelte sich das Gallus zu einem von Industrie- und Handwerksbetrieben geprägten Stadtteil. Für die Arbeiter entstanden hier in der 1. Hälfte des 20. Jahrhunderts unter Stadtbaurat Ernst May die Hellerhof- und die Friedrich-Ebert-Siedlung. 2001 wurde das Viertel in das Bund-Länder-Programm ‚Stadtteile mit besonderem Entwicklungsbedarf – die Soziale Stadt' aufgenommen und mit Modernisierungen begonnen.

Unser Rundgang startet an der Haltestelle ‚Rebstöcker Straße'. Wir folgen zunächst der Mainzer Landstraße nach Westen, unter der Eisenbahnbrücke hindurch. Gegenüber eines Autohauses biegen wir links in die Ackermannstraße ab und erreichen an der Einmündung der Cordierstraße unser erstes Ziel: Durch einen gut sichtbaren Bild- und Texthinweis an der Querwand bildet das 2011 fertig gestellte Mehrfamilienhaus in der **Ackermannstraße 41 b–d** den Eingang zur Friedrich-Ebert-Siedlung. Das viergeschossige *Passivhaus* mit Staffelgeschoß ersetzt eine Wohnzeile aus der Nachkriegszeit und fügt sich nahtlos in das städtische Bild ein. Der hoch wärmegedämmte Mauerwerksbau ermöglicht eine große Behaglichkeit bei minimalem Energie-

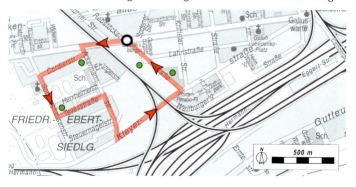

The Gallus Tour

After the construction of the main railway station in 1888, Gallus became a district dominated by industry and craft. During the first half of the 20th Century, under the tenure of city planner Ernst May, the Hellerhof and Friedrich Ebert estate were developed for the workers. In 2001, the district was included in the federal-state programme, 'Districts with Special Development Needs – the Social City'. Modernisations are progressing.

The tour begins at the tram stop 'Rebstöcker Straße'. Follow the Mainzer Landstraße westwards, passing under the railway bridge. Opposite a car dealership, turn left into Ackermannstraße and at the junction with Cordierstraße we reach the first point of interest. Writing on the apartment building **Ackermannstraße 41 b–d**, which was designed for community living, indicates the entrance to the Friedrich Ebert estate. In 2011, a *'Passive House'* was built which fits seamlessly into the urban image. It is accessible by three stairways which each lead to 10 apartments with unhindered access. The highly insulated, modern masonry construction provides comfort with low energy consumption. The rear, landscaped garage

> **Gallus:**
> Former field on the west boundary of the medieval city of Frankfurt and site of the gallows, which for almost five centuries served as a place of execution. The name derives from the gallows watch tower (Galluswarte), one of four medieval towers of the city. Only from the end of the 18th Century, does the name refer to the Holy Gallus.

> A *‚Passive House'* is a dwelling which is highly insulated and consequently does not need a conventional heating system. Heat energy is provided by the sun and also by body heat and that of technical appliances.

Ackermannstraße 41 b–d

1 | Gallus

Tevesstraße 36–54:

Bauherr/Client
ABG Frankfurt Holding GmbH

Architekt/Architect
faktor 10 Gesellschaft für Siedlungs- und Hochbauplanung mbH, Darmstadt

Baujahr/Year of construction
2004–2006

Nutzfläche/Useful area
Vergrößerung von 2.817 auf 3.775 m² Hauptnutzfläche/Increased from 2.817 to 3.775 m²

Tevesstraße 36–54:

Geschosswohnungen aus 1950er Jahren auf Passivhausstandard saniert – Energieverbrauch um 92% reduziert

Energetisches Niveau
| Zertifiziertes Passivhaus
| Auszeichnung als ‚Green Building Frankfurt' in 2009

Nutzung (erneuerbarer) Energien
| Erneuerung der Installationen
| Solarthermische Brauchwasserbereitung
| Lüftungsanlage mit Wärmerückgewinnung
| Natürliche Lüftung und Belichtung

Tevesstraße 36–54

verbrauch. Das Projekt wurde mit Mitteln aus dem familien- und seniorengerechten Mietwohnungsbauprogramm der Stadt Frankfurt gefördert. Es umfasst 30 Wohnungen, die barrierefrei erschlossen werden. Das rückwärtige, begrünte Tiefgaragendach dient als Gemeinschaftsbereich. Wir laufen die Cordierstraße bis zu ihrem anderen Ende. Das inzwischen aufgefrischte Areal prägen Wohnzeilen aus der Wiederaufbauzeit: Rund 50% der Siedlung gingen 1944 im Krieg verloren. 1947 bis 1950 wurden die Bauten größtenteils auf den ursprünglichen Grundrissen mit leicht modernisierten Fassaden wieder errichtet. Außergewöhnlich sind die im Verhältnis zum Straßenniveau abgesenkten Grün- und Hofflächen zwischen den Gebäuden. Aktuell wird hier ein Haus mit 17 Wohnungen gebaut, das mehr Energie erzeugen soll, als für die Versorgung der Bewohner notwendig ist.

Wir biegen links in die Sondershausenstraße ein. An der Evangelisch-Lutherischen Gemeinde und den Fußballplätzen vorbei gelangen wir zu den Wohnzeilen in der Tevesstraße. Gebäude aus den 1950er Jahren erfüllen oft nicht mehr die heutigen Ansprüche an Komfort und Gestaltung. Das Projekt in der **Tevesstraße 36–54** zeigt erstmals, dass eine hochenergetische Sanierung im sozialen Wohnungsbau realisierbar

roof can be used jointly by the occupants. Now go along the Cordierstraße to the end. Approximately 50% of the estate had been destroyed in 1944. From 1947 to 1950 the buildings were reconstructed, mostly according to the original plans, with slightly modernised facades. It is now characterized by four-storey residential buildings. The park area and courtyards between the buildings, which are lower than street level, are unusual. Currently an 'Energy Plus House' is being built containing 17 apartments. It can produce more energy than is required for the needs of the inhabitants. Turn left into Sondershausenstraße; pass the Evangelical Lutheran Church and the soccer fields to reach the next stop. This is marked by a change of colour from red to yellow on the first row of houses on the left hand side.

Buildings from the 1950s often do not meet more modern standards of comfort and design. The project in **Tevesstraße 36–54** shows that high-energy retrofitting of social housing can be feasible. Proven measures from modern building methods – highly insulated, tight building casing and controlled ventilation –reduce the annual energy consumption of 220 kWh/m² to 17.5 kWh/m². Solar panels on

Tevesstraße 36–54:

Apartments from the 1950s, renovated to Passive House standards – reduced energy consumption by 92%

Energetic Level
| *Certified passive house*
| Awarded as *'Green Building Frankfurt'* in 2009

Use (renewable) energy
| Renewal of installations
| Solar thermal hot water production
| Ventilation system with *heat recovery*
| Natural ventilation and light

Tevesstraße 36–54

Gallus

Tevesstraße 36–54:
Besonderheit, Tipp
Das Projekt wurde durch die Deutsche Energie Agentur als Pilotprojekt im Rahmen der Studie ‚Niedrigenergiehaus im Bestand' gefördert. Die begleitende Forschung übernahmen das Passivhaus Institut, das Institut Wohnen und Umwelt GmbH (IWU) und das Fraunhofer-Institut.

ist. Die im Neubau bewährten Maßnahmen – stark gedämmte, dichte Gebäudehülle und kontrollierte Wohnungslüftung – reduzieren den jährlichen Heizenergieverbrauch von 220 kWh/m² auf 17,5 kWh/m². Solarkollektoren auf den Dächern unterstützen die Warmwasserbereitung. Die Energie für Warmwasser wurde so um 40% vermindert. Die ehemals dreigeschossigen Gebäude wurden mit einem Holzleichtbau um eine Etage aufgestockt und bieten nun 56 zwischen 45 und 100 m² große Wohnungen.

Wir schlendern die Tevesstraße mit Blick auf die Skyline entlang. Dabei entdecken wir den historischen Teil der Friedrich-Ebert-Siedlung, die 1930 errichtet wurde. An der Ackermannstraße halten wir uns rechts und folgen ihr – unter Platanen – bis zur Kleyerstraße. Ab hier ist der Charakter des Gallus von großen, mehrgeschossigen Bürogebäuden bestimmt. Das Avaya-Firmengelände links und das ‚TELEHOUSE' rechts, unter Versorgungsrohren und zwei Eisenbahnbrücken hindurch, erreichen wir die Rebstöcker Straße 86.

Ordnungsamt:
Geothermie zur Gebäudeheizung und -kühlung

Seit Mai 2009 fasst das **Ordnungsamt** hier einige der größten Bereiche der Stadtverwaltung für die Bürger zentral zusammen – wie die Ausländerbehörde, die Stadtpolizei und das Fundbüro. Auch das Servicezentrum Rund ums Auto (Kfz-Zulassung, Bewohnerparken, etc.), Am Römerhof 19, gehört dazu. Der Stahlbetonbau mit teilweiser Natursteinverkleidung verbindet mit seiner Spiral-Bandstruktur die städtebauliche Umgebung und ermöglicht eine Kombination von Verdichtung und Offenheit mit entsprechender Belichtungsqualität. Das skulpturale, horizontal geschichtete und vorwiegend in klassischem schwarz-weiß-Kontrast gestaltete Gebäude deckt über 90% seines Energiebedarfs für Heizung/Kühlung und Warmwasser aus Geothermie. Dadurch verringern sich die Betriebs-

Ordnungsamt:
Bauherr/Client
Rebstöcker Str. GmbH & Co.KG, c/o OFB Projektentwicklung GmbH
Architekt/Architect
Meixner Schlüter Wendt Architekten, Frankfurt
Baujahr/
Year of construction
2006–2009
Nutzfläche/
Useful area
36.798 m²

the roofs augment the hot water supply. The energy requirement for hot water has thus been reduced by 40%. The former three-storey building has been built up with a lightweight timber additional level such that a total of 56 apartments from 45 to 100m² in floor area are now available.

Stroll along Tevesstraße overlooking the Frankfurt skyline. This is the historical part of the Friedrich-Ebert-estate, built in 1930. At Ackermannstraße keep right and follow it – under sycamore trees – to Kleyerstraße. From here Gallus is dominated by large, multi-story office buildings. Pass the Avaya premises on the left and the 'TELEHOUSE' on the right, passing under supply pipes and two railway bridges, we reach Rebstöcker Straße No. 86.

Since May 2009, the **Ordnungsamt** (local authority) in Gallus has centralised some of the major areas of the city administration – such as the immigration office, the city police, the

Tevesstraße 36–54:

Characteristic, tip

The project was promoted by the German Energy Agency, as a pilot project in the study 'Low-energy Homes'. The accompanying research was carried out by the Passive House Institute, the Institute for Housing and Environment (IWU) and the Fraunhofer Institute.

Ordnungsamt:

Geothermal heating and cooling of the building

Ordnungsamt

1 | Gallus

Ordnungsamt:

Energetisches Niveau
| *EnEV* 2002/04

Nutzung (erneuerbarer) Energien
| Geothermie: Erdwärmesonden
| Natürliche Belüftung und Belichtung

Ordnungsamt

Ordnungsamt:

Besonderheit, Tipp
Die Caféteria im Erdgeschoss ist öffentlich zugänglich.

Tevesgelände:
Wenn Sie im Startorante Ausbildungsrestaurant essen, erhalten Sie bei Vorlage dieses Reiseführers einen kostenfreien Softdrink. Folgen Sie einfach den Schildern:

Startorante
Rebstöcker Straße 49c
Tel.: 069-17 30 95 48 10
Montag bis Freitag
9.30 – 15.00 Uhr

kosten im Vergleich zu herkömmlichen Lösungen sowie die CO_2-Emmissionen erheblich. Die geologischen Gegebenheiten vor Ort ließen den Einsatz von Erdwärmesonden in Verbindung mit *Wärmepumpen* zu. In einem Zeitraum von vier Wochen entstand 2007 auf über 9.000 m² eines der größten Erdsondenfelder in Frankfurt. Die Bohrungen für insgesamt 112 Wärmesonden mit einem *Sole/Sole*-System reichen bis in 85 m Tiefe. Durch abwechselndes Verdampfen, Verdichten und Entspannen eines Kältemittels wird der aus dem Erdreich kommenden *Sole* Wärme entzogen und an den Heizkreislauf des Bürohauses abgegeben: Sie dient im Sommer zum Kühlen, im Winter zum Heizen.

Wir lassen das Amt rechts von uns und begeben uns entlang der Rebstöcker Straße zum **Gelände der ehemaligen Bremsenfabrik von Alfred Teves** auf der linken Seite. Seit 2005 haben sich in modernisierten Bauten des jahrelang brachliegenden Gebiets neue Nutzer angesiedelt: Träger beruflicher Bildung und Beschäftigung, Künstlerateliers, das Günes Theater sowie ein Box- und Tischtennis-Camp. Diese und weitere Initiativen haben das Gallus zum Dienstleistungszentrum mit Kulturadressen gewandelt.

Wir folgen der Rebstöcker Straße nun bis zum Ausgangspunkt.

lost property office and the automobile service centre, at Römerhof 19, which deals with all car matters (vehicle registration, residential parking, etc.). The reinforced concrete building with partial stone cladding and spiral ribbon structure creates an impression of openness. It derives over 90% of its energy for heating/cooling and hot water from geothermal sources. This reduces the operational costs compared to traditional solutions and significantly reduces CO_2 emissions. The geological conditions on site allowed the use of probes in conjunction with *heating pumps* for the detached building. In 2007 one of the largest fields of geothermal probes in Frankfurt was built on 9,000m². The drill holes for a total of 112 thermal probes with a *brine/brine* system extend to a depth of 85m. By alternate evaporation, compression and expansion of a refrigerant, the *brine* heat coming out of the ground is extracted and delivered to the heating circuit of the office building: It is used for cooling in summer.

Leaving the local authority offices to the right continue along Rebstöcker Straße to the site of the **former brakes factory of Alfred Teves** on the left. Since 2005 the industrial area, which lay abandoned for years, has been transformed. Sponsors of vocational training and employment, artists' studios, the Günes Theater and a boxing and table tennis camp have become established in modernised, well-developed buildings. These and other initiatives have thus converted Gallus sustainably into a centre of service with cultural flair.

We follow the Rebstöcker Straße back to the start of the tour.

Ordnungsamt:

Energetic Level
| *EnEV* 2002/04

Use (renewable) energy
| Geothermal heat: Borehole heat exchangers
| Natural ventilation and light

Ordnungsamt:

Characteristic, tip
The cafeteria on the ground floor is open to the public.

Teves premises:
If you eat in the restaurant Startorante you will get a free soft drink on presentation of this guide. Just follow the appropriate signs on the premises to:

Startorante
Rebstöcker Straße 49c

Phone: 069-17309 548 10

Monday to Friday
9.30 am – 3.00 pm

2 | Sachsenhausen

> Sachsenhausen heißt in Frankfurter Mundart „Dribb de Bach", also „drüben, jenseits des Flusses". „Hibb de Bach" („diesseits des Flusses") bezeichnet die nördliche Seite des Mains mit der Innenstadt.

Minimum Impact House:
Nachhaltige, vertikale Raumentfaltung auf städtischer Restfläche

Das Haus kann nach vorheriger Anmeldung besichtigt werden. Bitte wenden Sie sich an:
Dipl.-Arch. ETH Hans Drexler M. Arch. (Dist.)
Tel.: 069-962 06 234
E-Mail: drexler@dgj.eu

Minimum Impact House:

Bauherr/Client
Hans Drexler

Architekt/Architect
Drexler Guinand Jauslin Architekten GmbH, Frankfurt am Main

Baujahr/
Year of construction
2007–2008

Nutzfläche/Useful area
154 m²

Route Sachsenhausen – Mainufer – Westhafen

Sachsenhausen gehört seit dem Mittelalter zum Stadtgebiet Frankfurt. Im frühen 12. Jahrhundert ließen sich Ministerialen der Pfalz am südlichen Mainufer nieder, woran die Große und Kleine Rittergasse im alten Ortskern erinnern. Im 2. Weltkrieg wurde Sachsenhausen zu etwa 40% zerstört. Der nördliche Teil ist heute relativ dicht bebaut, der südliche vom Stadtwald geprägt.

Unsere Tour startet an der U-Bahnstation ‚Schweizer Platz'. Wir folgen der Oppenheimer Landstraße in nordöstlicher Richtung bis zur Gartenstraße, wo wir uns rechts halten. Auf Höhe des Oppenheimer Platzes, einem kleinen Park mit Brunnen und Spielplatz, kommt links die **Walter-Kolb-Straße 22** ins Blickfeld.

Das **Minimum Impact House** schafft aus einem innerstädtischen Fragment mit 29 m² Grundfläche einen fünffach größeren Nutzbereich. Es besitzt eine vollständige *Ökobilanz*, hohe architektonische Qualität und kann flexibel bespielt werden. Darüber hinaus machen die extreme Reduktion des Energiebedarfs sowie die Deckung des verbleibenden aus *erneuerbaren* Quellen den fünfgeschossigen Holztafelbau – einer der ersten in Deutschland – zu einem Vorbild für eine neue, ganzheitliche Optimierung. Der Prototyp ergänzt den Blockrand der umgebenden Gründerzeit-

Minimum Impact House

Sachsenhausen | 2

Tour Sachsenhausen – River Main – West Harbour

Sachsenhausen has been part of Frankfurt since the middle Ages. Palatine Ministries settled on the southern bank of the river Main in the early 12th century and the Große und Kleine Rittergasse in the old centre are redolent of this period. During the 2nd World War about 40% of Sachsenhausen was destroyed. Now much of the South is covered by woodland, the 'Stadtwald', whereas the North is densely built.

Our tour starts at the underground station 'Schweizer Platz'. Follow the Oppenheimer Landstraße in a North-Easterly direction to Gartenstraße, keeping to the right. At the Oppenheimer Platz, a small park with a fountain and a playground, number **22 Walter-Kolb-Straße** can be seen on the left.

The **Minimum Impact House,** which with 29m² of inn city urban space can create an area for use which is five times the norm. It is *ecologically balanced*, of high architectural quality and its use is flexible. It is a prototype which complements with its modernity the area surrounding it dating from the 19th century. With its facade it expresses the verticality and multiple layers of the urban environment.

Continuing the walk with a view of the

> **Sachsenhausen** is called in local dialect "Dribb de Bach", which means across the river in relation to the city centre.

> **Minimum Impact House:**
> Sustainable, vertical space development of small-scale available urban space
>
> By prior appointment the house can be visited individually. Please contact:
> Dipl.-Arch. ETH Hans Drexler M. Arch. (Dist.)
> Phone: 069-962 06 234
> E-Mail: drexler@dgj.eu

Minimum Impact House:

Energetisches Niveau
| Passivhaus
| Auszeichnung als ‚Green Building Frankfurt' in 2009

Nutzung (erneuerbarer) Energien
| Solarthermie für Warmwasser
| Regenwassernutzung
| Natürliche Lüftung und Belichtung
| Lüftungsanlage mit Wärmerückgewinnung
| Bezug von Ökostrom

Besonderheit, Tipp
| Einsatz nachwachsender Rohstoffe
| Ganzheitliche Optimierung des Energieverbrauchs – Nutzen von Standortqualitäten

---

Hier trinkt man sein ‚Stöffche' (Apfelwein) aus dem ‚Gerippten' (Apfelweinglas). Dazu gibt es Frankfurter Spezialitäten wie Rindfleisch mit Grüner Soße.

In den 1920er Jahren lebte und arbeitete **Paul Hindemith** im Kuhhirtenturm. In dem Gebäude werden seit 2011 Exponate zu dem Komponisten ausgestellt. Im Dachgeschoss gibt es einen Konzertsaal.

---

bebauung zeitgemäß. Mit seinen Fassaden greift er die Vertikalität und Mehrschichtigkeit des städtebaulichen Kontexts auf.

Wir laufen die Straße mit Blick auf die **Deutschordenskirche** weiter. Links in der **Schellgasse 8** entdecken wir das älteste erhaltene Fachwerkhaus Frankfurts, erbaut 1291/92. Wir gehen die Elisabethenstraße bis zur Paradiesgasse und stehen am Beginn von Alt-Sachsenhausen. Zwischen den Häusern hindurch würden wir die **Kleine Rittergasse** und die **Klappergasse** erreichen, wo sich eine urige Apfelwein-Wirtschaft an die andere reiht.

Wir halten uns links und gehen über das Kopfsteinpflaster der Paradiesgasse auf den **Kuhhirtenturm** zu, hinter dem sich Frankfurts Jugendherberge befindet. In dem schmalen Sträßchen mit kleinem Platz, Brunnen und Fachwerkhäusern fühlen wir uns in alte Zeiten versetzt. Im Zuge der Stadtbefestigung 1490 wurde der Turm, auch Elefant genannt, als Wehrbau am Mainufer errichtet.

Links weitet sich die Große Rittergasse zu einem Platz. An ihn grenzt der **Frankensteiner Hof**, ein ursprünglicher Adelssitz. Dieser wurde im Krieg zerstört und an seiner Stelle in den 1950er Jahren ein städtisches Amt errichtet, das nach einem Wettbewerb in 2002 zu Sozialrathaus, Wohnungen und Ateliers umgenutzt wurde. Seit 2008 folgt ein neues, ziegelrot verputztes viergeschossiges Haus mit neun öffentlich geförderten Mietwohnungen dem Straßenverlauf. Es öffnet sich mit Loggien und Privatgärten nach Süden. Seine schmalen Giebel und spitzen Dächer greifen die Kleinteiligkeit des Viertels auf.

Wir verlassen das Quartier und haben das **Ikonenmuseum** nun links von uns. Es befindet sich im Deutschordenshaus, dem östlichen Abschluss des Frankfurter Museumsufers. An der Kreuzung wechseln wir die Straßenseite und

Sachsenhausen | 2

Kuhhirtenturm

Frankensteiner Hof

'**Deutschordenskirche**' we discover on the left number **8 Schellgasse**, the oldest preserved timber framed building in Frankfurt, built in 1291/92. After walking down Elisabethenstraße to Paradiesgasse we reach the beginning of Alt-Sachsenhausen. If we walked in between the houses to the **Kleine Rittergasse** and **Klappergasse** we would find rows and rows of quaint apple wine inns.

But we keep to the left walking over the cobblestones in the Paradiesgasse towards the **Kuhhirtenturm**, behind which is Frankfurt's youth hostel. In this narrow street with its little square, the fountain and the timber framed houses one feel removed to a former age. During the building of the city's fortifications in 1490 the tower, also called 'The elephant', was erected. On the left the Große Rittergasse opens out into a square. There is the **Frankensteiner Hof**, a former seat of the nobility. After a competition in 2002 the municipal office is now used by offices for the local council, apartments and studios. Towards the South there are loggias and private gardens. The narrow gabled and roofs reflect the diversity of this quarter.

After leaving this district the **Ikonenmuseum**, the museum of icons, is on our left. It is located in the Deutschordenshaus at the Eastern end

---

Minimum Impact House:

Energetic Level
| *Passive House*
| Awarded as *'Green Building Frankfurt'* in 2009

Use (renewable) energy
| Solar energy for hot water
| Rainwater utilisation
| Natural ventilation and lighting
| Ventilation system with *heat recovery*
| Usage/Purchase of green electricity

Characteristic, tip
| Use of renewable raw materials
| Integrated optimization of energy consumption – Use of location qualities

---

Here one drinks 'Stöffche' (apple wine) out of the 'Gerippten' (typical apple wine glass) and eats specialties from Frankfurt like beef with 'Grüne Soße' (a cold herbal sauce).

In the 1920s Paul Hindemith lived and worked in Kuhhirtenturm.
Since 2011 exhibits of the composer are on display. There is a concert room in the attic.

2 | Sachsenhausen

> Ein Staatskirchenvertrag verpflichtet die Stadt seit 1830, alle neun Kirchen in der City und die Dreikönigskirche zu unterhalten. In diesem findet zu den vier Hochfesten des Kirchenjahres das traditionelle Frankfurter Stadtgeläute statt.

> Das Museumsufer ist einer der wichtigsten Standorte für Museen in Deutschland und bietet eine spannende Gestaltung: In den 1980er Jahren wurden historische Bürgerhäuser entkernt und zeitgemäß ausgestattet. Daneben entstanden zahlreiche Neu- und Erweiterungsbauten von international bedeutenden Architekten.
> Informationen zu den Museen finden Sie im Service-Teil auf den Seiten 134 und 135.

blicken auf die **Alte Brücke**, die 1222 erstmals erwähnt wurde. Mehr als 18 Mal zerstört, erhielt sie ihre heutige Gestalt 1926. Nachdem 1945 der Mittelteil gesprengt worden war, wurde dieser 1965 durch eine stählerne Kastenbrücke ersetzt. Außerdem sehen wir die Maininsel, auf der sich seit 2006 die Ausstellungshalle ‚**Portikus**' befindet. Wir schlendern das Mainufer unter Platanen entlang und erkennen linker Hand die **Dreikönigskirche** aus rotem Mainsandstein. Der neugotische Bau wurde 1880 nach einem Entwurf von Dombaumeister Franz Josef Denzinger fertig gestellt. Vom Inneren aus sind die Glasfenster zu bewundern, die Charles Crodel 1956 schuf.

Wir folgen dem Sachsenhäuser Ufer. Vor uns sehen wir den **Eisernen Steg**, eine Fußgängerbrücke, die Sachsenhausen mit der Frankfurter Altstadt verbindet. Wir befinden uns jetzt auf dem Schaumainkai und erreichen links die **Villa Metzler**, eine der ersten im 19. Jahrhundert hier erbauten Bürgervillen, und den **Richard Meier-Bau**. Beide Gebäude gehören zum **Museum Angewandte Kunst**. Dessen Sanierung soll zukünftig rund 20% Energie einsparen: Die Wärmedämmung bei Fassaden und Dach wurden verbessert, die Doppelglas-Elemente abgedichtet und außen liegende Rollos angebracht. So muss im Sommer weniger klimatisiert wer-

Museum Angewandte Kunst

Sachsenhausen | 2

of the Frankfurt Museum Embankment. At the junction we cross the road and look at the **'Alte Brücke'**, the old bridge first mentioned in 1222, destroyed more than 18 times and in its present form since 1926. In 1945 the middle section was blown up, this was replaced by a steel girder bridge in 1965.

One also can see an island in the river Main on which the exhibition hall **'Portikus'** was built in 2006. Strolling along the Main embankment under sycamore trees and see the **Dreikönigskirche** on the left, which had been built with red Main sandstone in 1880 in a neo gothic style designed by the cathedral master builder Franz Josef Denzinger. Stained glass windows by Charles Crodel were added 1956.

Continuing the 'Sachsenhäuser' embankment we come to a foot bridge, the **'Eiserne Steg'**, which joins Sachsenhausen with Frankfurt's old town. We are now on the Schaumainkai, on the left is **Villa Metzler**, one of the first patrician villas built in the 19th Century, and the **Richard Meier-Bau**. Both buildings are part of the **Museum Angewandte Kunst (Museum of Applied Arts)**. Their refurbishment will save about 20% of energy in the future: thermal wall and roof insulation were improved, double glazing elements sealed and external blinds mounted. Thus, less air conditioning will be necessary in the summer. Constant room temperature is now regulated automatically.

Walking towards the Untermainbrücke we pass the **Weltkulturen Museum (Museum of World Cultures)**, the **Deutsche Filmmuseum (German Film Museum)**, the **Deutsche Architekturmuseum (German Architecture Museum)** and the **Museum für Kommunikation (Museum of Communication)**. On the opposite river bank is the **Jüdische Museum (Jewish**

> A state church contract obliges the city, since 1830, to maintain all nine churches in the city and the Dreikönigskirche. The traditional city bells of Frankfurt chime at the four solemnities of the liturgical year.

> The Museumsufer is one of the most important locations for museums in Germany and offers an exciting design: In the 1980s, historic town houses were gutted and fitted with contemporary furnishings. In addition, numerous new buildings and extensions were created by internationally renowned architects.
> For information on the museums, see the service section on the pages 134 and 135.

Mainufer/River bank

Städel

> Das immer am letzten Augustwochenende stattfindende Museumsuferfest ist mit 3 Millionen Besuchern inzwischen die größte Veranstaltung im Rhein-Main-Gebiet.
>
> Ende April findet die ‚Nacht der Museen' statt, bei der Ausstellungshäuser in Frankfurt und Offenbach bis zum frühen Morgen geöffnet sind.

den. Eine konstante Raumtemperatur wird nun automatisch geregelt.

Richtung Untermainbrücke reihen sich nun das **Weltkulturen Museum**, das **Deutsche Filmmuseum**, das **Deutsche Architekturmuseum** sowie das **Museum für Kommunikation** aneinander. Direkt am gegenüberliegenden Mainufer liegen das **Jüdische Museum** und das **Historische Museum**.

Am Holbeinsteg befindet sich links das 1815 als bürgerliche Stiftung begründete **Städel Museum** sowie das **Städelsche Kunstinstitut**. Die 2012 eröffneten Gartenhallen sind ein lichtdurchfluteter, unterirdischer Neubau mit 195 kreisrunden Oberlichtern, der mit seinen 3.000 m² die Ausstellungsfläche des Museums verdoppelt. Der Raum wird durch seine elegant geschwungene Decke geprägt, die nur auf 12 Innenstützen ruht und nach außen ein begrüntes und begehbares Zeichen schafft. Auch das energetische Konzept ist bemerkenswert: Durch die kompakte Stahlbetonbauweise im Erdreich, die Wärme-/Kälteerzeugung mit Erdpendelspeicher und *Wärmepumpe* sowie die große innere Speichermasse kann ein für den Museumsbetrieb optimales Raumklima mit minimalem Energieaufwand erzielt werden. Im Städel sind nun 700 Jahre abendländischer Kunstgeschichte in ebenbürtigen Präsentationen erlebbar.

Wir laufen unter Platanen Richtung **Friedensbrücke** und kommen dabei links an der Villa mit idyllischem Park der **Liebieghaus Skulpturensammlung** sowie dem **Museum Giersch** vorbei. An der Bronze-Skulptur ‚Der Hafenarbeiter' (Constantin Meunier, 1890er Jahre) vorbei gehen wir bis zum rechten Treppenabgang der Brücke. Hier wechseln wir auf den Uferweg Richtung **Westhafen Tower**. Wegen seiner rautenförmigen Glasfassade wird er von den Frankfurtern auch ‚Geripptes' (Apfelweinglas)

Museum), the **Historische Museum (Historical Museum)**.

The **Städel Museum**, founded in 1815, and the **Städelsche Kunstinstitut** are located to the left of Holbeinsteg. An underground construction which 195 circular skylights is suffused with light, doubles the 3,000m² exhibition space of the Städel. Its elegantly curved ceiling rests on only 12 interior pillars creating outside a green accessible space. Its energy concept is remarkable: In this compact reinforced concrete underground construction an optimum climate for a museum can be created with minimum energy consumption due to the heating/cooling system using a *geothermal pump* and large internal storage capacity. 700 years of Western Art History can now be witnessed in the Städel on only one level.

Continuing the walk under the sycamores towards the **Friedensbrücke (peace bridge)** we pass on the left with the idyllic park the **Villa Liebieghaus** with its collection of sculptures and the **Museum Giersch**. Behind the bronze 'Der Hafenarbeiter' (Constantin Meunier, 1890s), we walk down some steps on the right of the bridge. Here we take the path on the embankment towards the **'Westhafen Tower'**. Its nickname 'Geripptes' reminds one of an apple wine glass because of its diamond-shaped glass facade. The rooms within the tower are square and the space between them and the outer wall contains conservatories. This energy-efficient office tower stands as the Eastern entree to a new urban district with apartments, offices, shops and restaurants which was developed in 1999, where the former inland port had been. Climbing up to the black stone steps and keeping left we find the 560m long and 75m wide harbour basin which is separated from the Main by a jetty with

The Museumsuferfest (museums festival) which always takes place on the last weekend in August is, with 3 million visitors, now the largest event in the Rhine-Main area.

End of April the event 'Nacht der Museen' takes place. Museums and exhibition halls in Frankfurt and Offenbach are open the whole night.

In unmittelbarer Nähe zum **Westhafen Tower** entsteht in der Speicherstraße das weltweit erste Aktiv-Stadthaus mit insgesamt 74 Wohnungen. Das Gebäude erzeugt über *Photovoltaik* auf dem Dach und an der Südfassade mehr Energie als für die Versorgung der Bewohner notwendig ist.

Westhafen/West Harbour

Westhafenkontor:

Qualitätsgeprüftes Passivhaus mit DGNB-Zertifizierung in Gold

Westhafenkontor:

Bauherr/Client
Westhafenkontor GmbH & Co. KG

Architekt/Architect
msm meyer schmitzmorkramer Architekten, Frankfurt am Main

**Baujahr/
Year of construction**
2010–2011

Nutzfläche/Useful area
3.051 m²

genannt. Das Innere besteht aus quadratischen Elementen. Die verbleibenden Flächen zur runden Außenhaut sind Wintergärten.

Der energieeffiziente Büroturm ist das östliche Entrée zu einem neuen Stadtquartier mit Wohnungen, Büros, Läden und Gastronomie. Dieses wurde ab 1999 auf dem Gebiet eines ehemaligen Binnenhafens entwickelt. Wenn wir die schwarze Natursteintreppe hinauf gehen und uns links halten, sehen wir das 560 m lange und 75 m breite Hafenbecken, das durch eine Mole vom Main getrennt ist. Darauf befinden sich 12 Wohnhäuser mit eigenen Bootsanlegern. Wir folgen dem Kopfsteinpflaster des Bachforellenwegs, bis er sich kurz vor der geschwungenen Fußgängerbrücke zur Mole zu einem Platz weitet. Wir wenden uns nach rechts und nutzen die Zanderstraße bis zur **Gutleutstraße**, in die wir links abbiegen. Auf dem Weg dahin erkennen wir moderne Bürogebäude. Nach wenigen Schritten erreichen wir die Nr. 191:

Das Frankfurter **Straßenverkehrsamt** bietet einen umfangreichen Service zum Thema Straßenverkehr, so zum Beispiel Informationen über den Betrieb verkehrstechnischer Anlagen, zum Großraum- und Schwerverkehr oder zur Radverkehrsplanung. Mit dem Bezug des **Westhafenkontors** unterstreicht die Stadt –

12 houses and their own landing stage. We walk on cobble stones along the Bachforellenweg until it widens out into a square just before the foot bridge. There we turn right and walk along Zanderstraße past modern office buildings to get to **Gutleutstraße** where we turn left.

After a few steps we come to the **Straßenverkehrsamt**, the department of transport. The Frankfurt Straßenverkehrsamt is a comprehensive service provider for everything to do with traffic on the roads, such as information on the operation of traffic engineering systems, the greater metropolitan area traffic and heavy loads traffic or on cycle path planning. The move into the **Westhafenkontor** underscores the city's environmental awareness: On the 1,600m² of land, a modern *Passive House* office has been erected. It is the first newly erected building in

Westhafenkontor:

Certified as Passive House and as DGNB Gold

In close proximity to the Westhafen Tower in Speicherstraße the world's first active-town house with a total of 74 apartments is currently under development. The building generates more energy than is necessary for the supply of the inhabitants due to *photovoltaic* mounted on the roof and the south facade.

Westhafen Tower

2 | Sachsenhausen

Westhafenkontor:

Energetisches Niveau
| DGNB-Zertifikat in Gold 2011 für Neubau Büro- und Verwaltungsgebäude
| Qualitätsgeprüftes Passivhaus 2012

Nutzung (erneuerbarer) Energien
| Geothermie/Luft mit Wärmepumpen
| Adiabatische und freie Kühlung
| Bauteilaktivierung zu Heiz- und Kühlzwecken

Besonderheit, Tipp
Das Gebäude kann im Rahmen von Führungen besichtigt werden. Nähere Informationen und Anmeldung: www.architekturimdialog.de

Westhafenkontor/Straßenverkehrsamt

übrigens seit 2008 als erste Stadt DGNB-Mitglied – ihr Umweltbewusstsein: Auf dem 1.600 m² großen Grundstück entstand ein modernes Büro-Passivhaus. Es ist der erste fertig gestellte Neubau in Frankfurt, der das höchste deutsche Gütesiegel für nachhaltiges Bauen erhielt. Der Stahlbetonbau mit Mauerwerksverblendung erzielt in allen Teilbereichen der DGNB-Zertifizierung überdurchschnittliche Werte, insbesondere in ökologischer und ökonomischer Hinsicht.

Neben den energetischen Aspekten sowie der ganzjährigen thermischen Behaglichkeit haben auch Faktoren wie die Qualitätssicherung der Bauausführung, die gelungene Dachgestaltung, der geringe Trinkwasserbedarf und das niedrige Abwasseraufkommen zu den guten Ergebnissen geführt. Der Primärenergiebedarf von 84,4 kWh/(m²a) ist für den Gewerbeimmobilienbau richtungsweisend. Das Gebäude aus sechs Obergeschossen, einem Technik- und einem Untergeschoss ist horizontal markant gegliedert. Mit seinen Proportionen fügt sich die klare kubische Bauform gleichzeitig gut in die vorhandene Stadtstruktur ein.

Wir gehen die Gutleutstraße Richtung Eisenbahnbrücke weiter. Die Bauten und Versorgungsrohre zeigen, dass wir uns nun in einem

Westhafenkontor/Straßenverkehrsamt

Frankfurt to receive the highest German quality seal for sustainable building. In addition to the energy aspects and the year-round thermal comfort, factors such as the quality assurance of the building construction, the successful roof design, low water requirements and the low volume of waste water have led to these good results. The primary energy demand of 84.4 kWh/(m²a) sets the guidelines for industrial building. The six-storey building with an additional technical floor and a basement is divided horizontally and is striking. Its proportions and the clear cubic design fit well into the existing urban structure.

We walk along Gutleutstraße towards the railway bridge. The buildings and supply pipes indicate that we are now moving into an industrial area.

To the left we arrive at the entrance to our next destination. The power station **HKW West** in its present form dates from the end of the 1980s. Fuelled by coal the new blocks 2 and 3 produce simultaneously up to 69 electrical MW and 105 thermal MW of energy. A sealed silo and transport system prevents the release of coal dust into the environment. The gas turbine in block 4 can also add up to 99 electrical MW at times of high demand. In a steam boiler

---

Westhafenkontor:

Energetic Level
- *DGNB* Certificate in Gold for the new office and administration building
- *Passive House*, certified in 2012

Use (renewable) energy
- Geothermy with *heat pumps*
- *Adiabatic* cooling system
- Thermal *component activation*

Characteristic, tip
There are guided tours of the building. Information and applications to: www.architekturimdialog.de

Heizkraftwerk West:

High efficiency of combined power and heat production

Heizkraftwerk West:

Betreiber
Mainova AG

Strom- und Wärmeerzeugung
Seit 1894

Primärenergieträger
Steinkohle und Erdgas

Erzeugungskapazität
Max. Strom 253 MW
Strom in *Kraft-Wärme Kopplung* 198 MW
Fernwärme 400 MW

Versorgung mit Fernwärme
Innenstadt, Uni-Klinikum, Deutschherrnufer, Messe Frankfurt

Fernheizmedium
Dampf/Heizwasser

Heizkraftwerk West:

Hohe Effizienz durch Kraft-Wärme-Kopplung

Heizkraftwerk West:

Besonderheit, Tipp
Kostenfreie, etwa zweistündige Führungen (Gruppen von 10 – 30 Personen) werden wochentags von 8.00– 18.00 Uhr nach Voranmeldung angeboten:

Besucherdienst der Mainova AG
Tel.: 0 69-213 27 945
E-Mail: fuehrungen@mainova.de
www.mainova.de

Industriegebiet bewegen. Linker Hand kommen wir zum Eingang unseres nächsten Ziels. Seine heutige Gestalt erhielt das **Heizkraftwerk (HKW) West** Ende der 1980er Jahre. Die neuen Blöcke 2 und 3 erbringen jeweils bis zu 69 MW elektrische und 105 MW thermische Leistung. In ihnen wird Steinkohle verfeuert. Ein geschlossenes Silo- und Transportsystem verhindert, dass Kohlestaub in die Umwelt gelangt. Die Gasturbine in Block 4 kann zusätzliche elektrische Spitzenlasten bis 99 MW abdecken. Das 500 °C heiße Rauchgas erzeugt in einem nachgeschalteten Kessel Dampf, der mit einer Leistung von 160 MW in das *Fernwärmenetz* der Innenstadt eingespeist wird. Das HKW West bildet dabei einen Verbund mit dem **HKW Mitte** und dem **HKW Messe**. Durch das Prinzip der *Kraft-Wärme-Kopplung* erreichen die Heizkraftwerke einen Brennstoffnutzungsgrad von 80% und mehr. Die Brenner der Kesselanlagen in den Blöcken 2 und 3 ermöglichen darüber hinaus eine schadstoffarme Verbrennung. Bei der Nachbehandlung werden dem Rauchgas Stickoxide, Schwefeldioxid und Staub entzogen. Dabei entsteht unter anderem ein Zuschlagstoff für Zement. Am Ende des Prozesses bleiben Wasser und Stickstoff mit einem Reststaubgehalt von 8 bis 10 mg/m³ (gesetzlicher Grenzwert 20 mg/m³) übrig. Wie alle Mainova-Heizkraftwerke arbeitet auch dieses auf höchstem umwelttechnischen Niveau. Zudem befindet sich eine Pilot-Forschungsanlage zur CO_2-Resorption mittels Algen auf dem Gelände: In zwei Becken, die mit algenhaltigem Wasser gefüllt sind, wird Rauchgas eingeleitet. Die Algen setzen 90% bis 95% des zugeführten CO_2 in Biomasse um und reduzieren somit den CO_2-Ausstoß des HKW.

Wir folgen dem Straßenverlauf zur Eisenbahnbrücke. Hier biegen wir links in den Fuß- und Radweg ‚Am Elektrizitätswerk' ab. An der **Main-**

exhaust gases at 500 °C produce up to 160 MW for the inner city *heating network*. The 3 power stations HKW West, **HKW Mitte**, and **HKW Messe** work together to achieve at least 80% fuel efficiency. The burners in blocks 2 and 3 make the transformation almost pollution free and with further treatment nitrogen dioxide, sulphur dioxide and dust are extracted. What remains is used amongst other things as an ingredient for cement production. At the end of the process water and nitrogen oxide remain with a pollutant content of 8 to 10 mg/m³ (the legal limit is 20 mg/m³). Like all Mainova power stations this one, too, is technically highly advanced and environmentally friendly. There is even a pilot research plant for the resorption of CO_2 using algae. Carbon dioxide is fed into two basins filled with water containing algae which converts between 90% and 95% of the carbon dioxide into bio mass thereby reducing further the carbon dioxide emission of the power station. Following the road to the railway bridge we turn left into the pedestrian and bicycle path 'Am

Heizkraftwerk West:

Operator
Mainova AG

Power and
heat production
Since 1894

Main energy producers
Coal and natural gas

Production capacity
Max. 253 MW electricity
Combined power and heat production of 198 MW
District heating 400MW

Supplied by district heating
Inner city, University hospital, the Deutschherrnufer estate, Trade fair Frankfurt

District heating
Steam and heated water

Heizkraftwerk (HKW) West

Algenversuchsanlage im HKW West/Algae pilot plant

Neckar-Brücke halten wir uns links, auf den Turm des denkmalgeschützten **Druckwasserwerks** zu. Der neoromanische Backsteinbau ist der einzig verbliebene Teil der ursprünglichen Hafen-Bebauung und Teil der Route Industriekultur Rhein-Main. Sein zentraler Maschinenraum dient jetzt als Gastraum. Das Gebäude wurde 2009 als ‚Denkmal des Jahres' ausgezeichnet. Es ist auch das erste Gebäude in Frankfurt mit der Kennzeichnung als Kulturdenkmal gemäß der Haager Konvention.

Von hier schlendern wir, den Main und an modernen Büro- und Wohngebäuden entlang, zurück zur Friedensbrücke. Alternativ nehmen wir den Bus 33. Wenn wir uns an der Brücke links zur Stadtmitte orientieren, erreichen wir den **Baseler Platz**. Auf seiner rechten Seite, zwischen Wilhelm-Leuschner-Straße und Gutleutstraße, liegen hinter dem ‚Oval' die **‚Baseler Arkaden'**, ein Niedrigenergiegebäude mit heller Natursteinverkleidung. Bei ihm sorgen großzügige Fensterflächen für eine natürliche Belichtung und Belüftung der Räume, Thermalwasser dient zum Heizen/Kühlen und die Wärme- und Kälteabgabe erfolgt über Thermoaktivdecken.

Die Friedensbrücke im Rücken, folgen wir der Baseler Straße und kommen zum Hauptbahnhof, dem Endpunkt der Route.

Elektrizitätswerk'. At the **Main-Neckar Bridge** we bear left and walk towards the spire of the listed **building of the high pressure waterworks**. The neo-romanesque brick building is the only remaining part of the initial development and part of the Route of Industrial Heritage Rhine-Main. The central engine room now serves as a guest room. In 2009 the building was awarded 'Monument of the Year'. It is also the first building in Frankfurt with the designation as a cultural monument under the Hague Convention.

From here we stroll along the River Main past modern office and residential buildings, back to the Friedensbrücke. Alternatively we can take bus number 33. If we keep left of the city centre at the bridge, we reach the **Baseler Platz**. Between Wilhelm-Leuschner-Straße and Gutleutstraße, to the right and behind the Oval is the **'Baseler Arkaden'**, a low-energy building with a bright natural stone cladding. Generous windows provide natural lighting and ventilation of the rooms, thermal water is used for heating/cooling and the heating and cooling provision takes place via thermo-active ceilings.

With the Friedensbrücke behind us, we follow the Baseler Straße and arrive at the main railway station, the end of our route.

Druckwasserwerk/Waterworks

3 | Westend

Das Bankenviertel erstreckt sich im Westend entlang der Bockenheimer Anlage, Taunusanlage und Mainzer Landstraße sowie den angrenzenden Teilen der Innenstadt und des Bahnhofsviertels. Die Konzentration von Bürohochhäusern ist in Deutschland einmalig. Bei dem in unregelmäßigen Abständen stattfindenden Wolkenkratzer-Festival können gegen Voranmeldung auch sonst nicht öffentliche Bereiche der Skyscraper besucht werden.

Das ‚TRIANON':

Bestandsimmobilie mit Spitzenwert bei LEED-Gold-Zertifizierung

Trianon:

Bauherr/Client
Bank für Gemeinwirtschaft

Architekt/Architect
Novotny Mähner Assoziierte, Offenbach, HPP Hentrich-Petschnigg & Partner und Albert Speer & Partner, Frankfurt am Main

Baujahr/
Year of construction
1989–1993

Nutzfläche/Useful area
66.000 m²

Route Westend Süd – Europaviertel – Westend Nord

Etwa Mitte des 19. Jahrhunderts wurde das **Westend** parzelliert und Straßen und Plätze nach Pariser Vorbild angelegt. Bis in die 1950er Jahre stellte es ein reines Wohngebiet mit meist viergeschossigen Häusern dar. Das 1960 erbaute und inzwischen wieder abgerissene Gebäude der Zürich-Versicherung war eines der ersten Hochhäuser in Frankfurt und das erste im Westend. Auf seinem Gelände steht heute der Opernturm. Vor allem entlang der Hauptachsen erfolgte in der 2. Hälfte des 20. Jahrhunderts eine intensivierte Bebauung mit vorwiegend Büronutzung.

Ausgangspunkt ist die S-Bahnstation ‚Taunusanlage'. Hier stehen wir direkt vor den beiden 155 m hohen **Türmen der Deutschen Bank**, auch ‚Soll' und ‚Haben' genannt. Die Stahlbetonskelettbauten mit vorgehängter Aluminium-Glasfassade wurden komplett saniert und bekamen beim ‚Internationalen Hochhaus Preis' der Stadt Frankfurt in 2012 eine besondere Anerkennung: Ohne die ursprüngliche Struktur aus dem Jahr 1984 zu verändern, wurden Nachhaltigkeit, Energieeffizienz und Nutzerkomfort erheblich gesteigert. So konnte der Energieverbrauch um 50%, der für Wasser um gut 70% und der CO_2-Ausstoß um fast 90% verringert werden. Zertifizierungen nach *LEED* (Platin) und *DGNB* (Gold) dokumentieren dies.

Wir lassen die Deutsche Bank rechts von uns und folgen der Mainzer Landstraße in südlicher Richtung. Hinter einem Gründerzeitbau sehen wir bereits unser nächstes Ziel mit der Nr. 16. Mit 186 m Höhe, einer repräsentativen Vorhangfassade aus Aluminium und der charakteristischen Dreiecksform zählt das **Trianon** zu den markantesten Wolkenkratzern der Frankfurter **Skyline** und des **Bankenviertels**. 2012 wurde der

Westend | 3

Tour Southern Westend – European Quarter – Northern Westend District

Around the mid-19th Century, the **Westend** district was divided into lots of streets and squares according to Parisian tradition. Until the 1950s, it was a residential area with mostly four-storey buildings. The Zurich Insurance building erected in 1960 was one of the first skyscrapers in Frankfurt and the very first in the Westend. The original building has been demolished in the meantime and the site has been replaced with another building, the Opernturm. In the 2nd half of the 20th Century, buildings with predominantly for office use were developed along the major roads of the district.

The starting point of our tour is the train station 'Taunusanlage'. The two 155m high **towers of the Deutsche Bank** in front of us are also known as 'Credit' and 'Debit'. The reinforced concrete

The financial district extends along the Bockenheimer Anlage, Taunusanlage und Mainzer Landstraße and the adjacent parts of the city centre and of the Bahnhofsviertel. In Germany the concentration of office building highrises is unique. During the Skyscraper Festival, held at irregular intervals, even Skyscrapers, which cannot otherwise be visited publicly, are accessible by prior appointment.

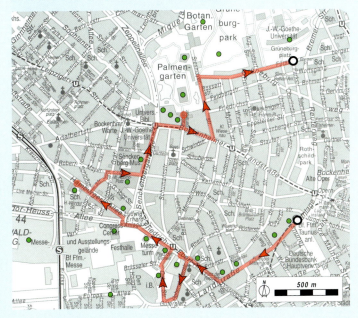

Trianon

Trianon:

Energetisches Niveau
| LEED-Zertifizierung in Gold 2012 für Kategorie ‚Existing Buildings'

Nutzung (erneuerbarer) Energien
| Einsatz innovativer und umweltfreundlicher Gebäudetechnik
| Natürliche Belichtung, Sonnenschutzverglasung
| Vollklimaanlage mit *Wärmerückgewinnung*
| Anschluss an das *Fernwärmenetz*

Besonderheit, Tipp
Repräsentativer Mittelpunkt des Gebäudes ist die 17 m hohe Lobby, die den Besucher mit viel Licht und Weite empfängt. Sie ist öffentlich zugänglich. Die integrierte Cafeteria lädt zu einem Zwischenstopp ein.

Immobilie das *LEED*-Gold-Zertifikat in der Kategorie ‚Existing Buildings' verliehen. Mit einer erreichten Punktzahl von 73 ist es eines der am besten bewerteten Bestandsgebäude Deutschlands. Während der zweijährigen Zertifizierungsphase wurde das Trianon vor allem hinsichtlich der Ressourcen- und Energieeffizienz optimiert und bewertet und dabei Maßnahmen zur dauerhaften Reduzierung des Energieverbrauchs implementiert. So ließen nachhaltige Entsorgungskonzepte, wassersparende Sanitärinstallationen und die gute Erreichbarkeit mit umweltfreundlichen Verkehrsmitteln das Gebäude punkten. Auch nach den Anforderungen der Energy Star-Kennzeichnung ist es als ‚hoch effizient' eingestuft. Der Grundriss des Trianon ist ein gleichseitiges Dreieck. Dreiseitige Pfeiler, die über das Dach hinausragen, rahmen die Ecken

Trianon

construction with a suspended aluminium glass facade has been completely renovated and in 2012 received special recognition from the city of Frankfurt, as part of the 'International High-rise Award'. This was awarded for several reasons; without changing the original structure dating from 1984, sustainability, energy efficiency and user comfort were considerably increased. Thus, energy consumption could be reduced by 50%, water consumption by at least 70% and CO_2 emissions by almost 90%. This is documented by *LEED* (Platinum) and *DGNB* (Gold) certifications.

We leave the Deutsche Bank to our right and follow the Mainzer Landstrasse in a southerly direction. Behind the 19th century style building we can see our next destination.

With a height of 186m, a representative aluminium facade and a characteristic triangular shape, the **Trianon** is one of the most striking skyscrapers of Frankfurt's **Skyline** and the **financial district**. In 2012 it was awarded the *LEED* Gold Certification in the category 'Existing Buildings'. With an overall score of 73, it is one of the top rated existing buildings in Europe. The Trianon was under the scrutiny of a certification committee for two years regarding its efficient use of resources and energy with lasting measures for the reduction of energy consumption being implemented. Plans for water saving sanitary installations, the removal of waste and easy access to environmentally friendly means of transport all helped to impress. The building attained the Energy Star Standard being granted the 'highly efficient' certification. The floor plan of the Trianon is an equilateral triangle. Tripartite pillars which protrude from the roof, frame the corners of the high-rise building. A highly visible upside-down pyramid appears to float between the pillars. The

The 'TRIANON':

Existing property with top values for LEED Gold Certification

Trianon:

Energetic Level
| *LEED* Gold Certificate in 2012 for category 'Existing Buildings'

Use (renewable) energy
| Use of innovative and environment-friendly building techniques
| Natural lighting and sun protection glazing
| Full air conditioning with *heat recovery*
| Connection to the *district heating* network

Characteristic, tip
Representative centre-piece of the building is 17m high lobby that greets the visitor with plenty of light and space. It is publicly accessible. The integrated coffee shop is ideal for a break.

3 | Westend

City Haus I, DZ-Bank:
Städtebauliche und energetische Modernisierung bei laufendem Betrieb

City Haus I, DZ-Bank:

Bauherr / Client
DVG Deutsche Vermögensverwaltungsgesellschaft mbH & Co. Objekt City Haus | KG

Architekt / Architect
Prof. Christoph Mäckler Architekten, Frankfurt am Main

**Baujahr /
Year of construction**
2008

Nutzfläche /Useful area
43.500 m²

Energetisches Niveau
Die Energiewerte der neuen Fassadengläser unterbieten die geforderten Werte der *EnEV* 2007 und sparen so jährlich rund 35 % des ursprünglichen Gesamtenergieaufwands ein, davon etwa 37 % bei der Heizung und gut 20 % bei der Kühlung.

Nutzung (erneuerbarer) Energien
| Natürliche Lüftung und Beleuchtung

des Hochhauses ein. Zwischen diesen schwebt eine auf den Kopf gestellte, weithin sichtbare Pyramide. Das Gebäude im **Westend** verfügt über 47 Obergeschosse. Der Bau wird über 3 Innenkerne sowie die umlaufende Stahlbetonlochfassade ausgesteift. Für die tragenden Stützen und Wände kam hochfester Beton B 85 zur Anwendung – und das erstmalig in Deutschland.

Aus dem Bahnhofsviertel ragen links die Glasfassade des **Skyper** und die Aluminium-Glasfassade des **Silver Tower** heraus. Der Silver Tower ist das einzige Gebäude in Frankfurt mit abgerundeten Ecken und wurde bis 2011 umfassend modernisiert. Auf unserem Weg entlang der Mainzer Landstraße passieren wir rechts das **Frankfurter Büro Center** und kommen zum **Westend Tower**, der wegen seiner Spitze auch Kronenhochhaus genannt wird. Davor steht die Skulptur ‚Inverted Collar and Tie' von Claes Oldenburg und Coosje van Bruggen von 1994.

Ein Stück weiter, am Platz der Republik, sehen wir rechts das **Gebäude der DZ-Bank** von 1975, das auch als ‚Selmi-Hochhaus' bekannt ist. Der 143 m hohe Stahlbeton-Skelettbau setzt sich aus zwei mittig angeordneten Treppenhauskernen sowie zwei gegeneinander versetzten scheibenförmigen Bürotrakten mit jeweils 40

City Haus I, DZ-Bank

City Haus I, DZ-Bank

building has 47 floors. The 3 inner cores of the reinforced concrete building are strengthened by its elevator shafts and stairwells. For first time in Germany high strength concrete B 85 was used to support the pillars and walls.

The glass facade of the **Skyper** and the aluminium glass facade of the **Silver Tower** stand out from the other buildings in the Bahnhofsviertel. The Silver Tower is the only building in Frankfurt with rounded corners and was extensively modernized until 2011. On our way along the Mainzer Landstrasse we pass on the right the **Frankfurt office centre** and come to the **Westend Tower**, which, due to its crest, is also known as 'Kronenhochhaus'. The sculpture, 'Inverted Collar and Tie' by Claes Oldenburg and Coosje van Bruggen from 1994, can be seen in front of this building.

City Haus I, DZ-Bank:
Urban and energy modernisation during normal working operations

City Haus I, DZ-Bank:
Energetic Level
The energy values of the new glass facade undercut the required values of *EnEV* 2007, saving annually about 35% of the original total energy expenditure, about 37% in heating and over 20% in cooling.

Use (renewable) energy
| Natural ventilation and lighting

Characteristic, tip
The new cladding/shell was as a facade element attached to the substructure of the existing facade – thermally separated and sun and soundproof glazing and insulated glass balustrade panels. To improve the comfort, a textile glare shield is installed and each second window can be opened.

3 | Westend

City Haus I, DZ-Bank:

Besonderheit, Tipp
Die neue Haut wurde als Elementfassade an die Unterkonstruktion der Bestandsfassade gehängt – thermisch getrennt und mit Sonnen-/Schallschutzverglasung und wärmegedämmten Glasbrüstungsverkleidungen. Zur Verbesserung der Behaglichkeit wurde ein textiler Blendschutz eingebaut und in jeder zweiten Fensterachse ein zu öffnender Lüftungsflügel.

Obergeschossen zusammen. Die Sanierung in 2008 wertete das City Haus I energetisch, optisch und städtebaulich auf. Dazu gehören die Ausbildung einer großzügigen Eingangshalle samt öffentlich zugänglicher Galerie am Platz der Republik, die gestalterische Betonung der Vertikalen sowie der Einsatz moderner Funktionsgläser mit hoher Licht- und geringer Wärmedurchlässigkeit. Die Fassadenelemente wurden bei laufendem Betrieb geschossweise ausgetauscht.

Wir lassen den Bau rechts von uns und kommen entlang der Friedrich-Ebert-Anlage am **Goethe-Gymnasium**, einem typischen 1950er Jahre Bau, vorbei. Seit 1993 besitzt die Schule eine *Photovoltaik*anlage, die hilft, jährlich 1,1 t CO_2 zu vermeiden. An der Kreuzung zur Rheinstraße wechseln wir auf die andere Seite.

Tower 185:
Städtebauliche Identität und energieoptimierter Bau

Tower 185:

Bauherr/Client
CA Immo Deutschland GmbH

Architekt/Architect
Prof. Christoph Mäckler Architekten, Frankfurt am Main

Baujahr/Year of construction
2008–2012

Nutzfläche/Useful area
100.000 m²

Tower 185

A little further on, at the Platz der Republik, we see on the right, the **building of the DZ-Bank** from 1975, which is also known as, 'Selmi-Building'. The 143m high reinforced concrete structure is composed of two centrally located stairwell cores and two staggered disk-shaped office wings each with a total of 40 storeys. The City House was renovated in 2008 leading to an upgrade in terms of energy, visual and urban design. The renovations include the creation of a spacious entrance hall, with a publicly available gallery adjacent to the Platz der Republik, an emphasis on vertical design and the use of modern industrial glass with high light and low heat conductivity. The facade elements were replaced storey by storey while normal working operations continued.

We leave the DZ-Bank on our right and pass the **Goethe-Gymnasium** on the Friedrich-Ebert-Anlage; this is a typical building of the 1950s. Since 1993 the school has had a *photovoltaic* system, which helps to prevent 1.1 tons of CO_2 annually. At the junction with the Rheinstraße we cross the road.

Tower 185 with its 50 floors forms the prelude to the **European quarter** beyond. Its perimeter block style harmonises well with the surroundings due to its clear structure; adopting the heights, material qualities and colours of neighbouring buildings. A pear-shaped plaza leads visitors to the entrance hall. The tower ensemble is a construction of composite reinforced concrete. Its supports are placed in the plane of the facade; hence, less energy penetrates into the building. In conjunction with the high-performance glazing in the aluminium facade and the sun shading of glass surfaces, due to facade projections, air conditioning is not necessary except in the areas of data centre servers.

3 | Westend

Tower 185:

Energetisches Niveau
- *LEED*-Zertifikat in Gold 2012 für Bürohochhaus, Neubau

Nutzung (erneuerbarer) Energien
- Energiesparende Flächenkühl- und Heizsysteme
- Nutzung von Regenwasser für Außenanlagen und WC-Spülung
- Natürliche Lüftung und Beleuchtung
- Über 25% begrünte Grundstücksfläche

Besonderheit, Tipp
Einsatz von Baumaterialien mit recycelten Anteilen (15–20%), regionalen Baustoffen (10–20%), schadstofffreien Farben, Beschichtungen und Dichtungsmaterialien. Die Energiewerte des Turms unterbieten die geforderten Werte der *EnEV* 2007 um mehr als 20%.

Die energieeffizienten Neubauten des Europaviertels und andere in diesem Buch vorgestellte Gebäude können Sie im Rahmen von Führungen besichtigen. Nähere Informationen und Anmeldung bei: Susanne Petry, Dipl. Ing. Arch. Architektur im Dialog Tel.: 0 69-66 57 59 70 E-Mail: petry@architekturimdialog.de

---

Mit 50 Geschossen bildet der **Tower 185** den Auftakt zum dahinter liegenden **Europaviertel**. Seine Blockrandbebauung fügt sich durch die klare Gliederung, die Übernahme von Höhen, Materialqualitäten und Farben der Nachbarbauten in die Umgebung ein. Ein tropfenförmiger Platz leitet den Besucher zur Eingangshalle. Das Turm-Ensemble ist in Stahlbeton-/Stahlbetonverbundbauweise errichtet. Seine Stützen befinden sich in der Ebene der Fassade: So dringt weniger Energie in das Gebäude ein. Unterstützt wird dies durch die Hochleistungsverglasung in der Aluminium-Fassade und die Verschattung der Glasflächen durch Fassadenvorsprünge, so dass bei dem Bürogebäude – außer bei den Serverbereichen des Rechenzentrums – keine Klimatisierung nötig ist.

Mit Blick auf die neugotische **Matthäuskirche** von 1905 gehen wir auf die Hohenstaufenstraße zurück, der wir bis zur Osloer Straße folgen. Geradeaus kämen wir in den 60 m breiten Boulevard der **Europa-Allee**. Mit dem **Europaviertel** wächst auf dem Gelände des ehemaligen Hauptgüterbahnhofs derzeit ein neues urbanes Quartier – vom Rebstockgelände entlang des Messegeländes bis zum Güterplatz und der Hellerhofsiedlung.

Wir wenden uns rechts dem östlichen Quartierseingang zu. Eine Besonderheit wird der öffentlich zugängliche Dachgarten des **Skyline Plaza** (Vorzertifikat *DGNB* Gold) werden, von wo aus der Besucher einen Blick über die Stadt genießen kann.

Kap Europa – der Name des Kongresszentrums in der Osloer Straße nimmt sowohl Bezug auf die klare Formensprache des Gebäudes selbst als auch auf seinen Standort im **Europaviertel**. Dieses zeichnet sich durch seine zukunftsweisenden Hotel- und Büroneubauten aus. Gleichzeitig bietet es hochwertige Stadtwohnungen und inter-

Westend | 3

Tower 185

Looking at the neo-Gothic **church of St. Matthew** from 1905 we go back towards Hohenstaufenstraße, which we follow to Osloer Straße. Straight ahead of us is the 60m wide boulevard of the **Europa-Allee**. Together with the **European district**, on the former site of the main freight depot, an additional urban quarter is currently in growth – from the Rebstock grounds along the exhibition centre grounds to Güterplatz and the Hellerhofsiedlung.

We turn right to the eastern entrance of the area. A special feature will be the publicly accessible roof garden of the **Skyline Plaza** (pre-certification *DGNB* gold), from where visitors can enjoy a view of the city.

Kap Europa – the name of the new conference centre in Osloer Straße refers both to the clear design of the building itself as well as its location in the **European quarter**. This is distinguished by its trend-setting hotel and newly built office buildings. At the same time, it provides high quality apartments and international gastronomy. The multi usage complex is complemented by the almost

Tower 185:
Urban identity and energy-optimized construction, about 100,000 m² of rentable space

Tower 185:
Energetic Level
| LEED Gold Certificate in 2012 for high-rise office building, in the category 'New Building'

Use (renewable) energy
| Energy efficient surface cooling and heating systems
| Using rainwater for outdoor facilities and toilet flushing systems
| Natural ventilation and lighting
| About 25% of vegetated land

Characteristic, tip
The building material used consists of 15–20% recycled material, 10–20% from regional origin, paints, coatings and sealing materials free of hazardous substances. The towers energetic level is more than 20% lower than the values required by *EnEV* 2007.

3 | Westend

Kap Europa:
Erstes Kongressgebäude weltweit mit DGNB-Vorzertifikat in Gold

Kap Europa:

Bauherr / Client
Congress Centrum Skyline Plaza GmbH & Co. KG

Architekt / Architect
Dipl.-Ing. Architekt Klaus Lenz, Hamburg

Baujahr / Year of construction
2012–2014

Nutzfläche/Useful area
7.700 m²

Energetisches Niveau
| Nachhaltigkeitsansprüche an Bau und Betrieb der *DGNB*, Vorzertifikat 2012
| Unterschreiten *EnEV* 2009 um bis zu 30%

Nutzung (erneuerbarer) Energien
| Einsatz umweltverträglicher Materialien
| Hoher Tageslichtanteil und innovatives Beleuchtungskonzept mit LED-Anteil
| *Bauteilaktivierung*: Betonkern für Kühlung
| Hochwertig gestaltetes Gründach

Besonderheit, Tipp
Direkte Nachbarschaft zum Shoppingcenter Skyline Plaza und ideale ÖPNV-Anbindung.
www.kapeuropa.de

Kap Europa

nationale Gastronomie. Die Nutzungsmischung wird durch den fast 60.000 m² großen Europagarten ergänzt. Das Kongresshaus bildet zusammen mit dem benachbarten Einkaufszentrum **Skyline Plaza** ein Highlight im Europaviertel. Der Bau hat im April 2012 begonnen. Die Inbetriebnahme ist für 2014 vorgesehen. Die Stahlbetonkonstruktion ergänzt das Raumangebot des seit 1997 bestehenden Congress Centers der Messe Frankfurt und bietet auf vier Veranstaltungsebenen einen Saal für 1.000 Personen, einen teilbaren Saal für 600 Personen sowie 12 weitere, partiell teilbare, Tagungsräume. Das Kap Europa übernimmt eine Vorbildfunktion hinsichtlich ökologisch- und sozialverträglicher Bauweisen und des Betriebs. Dies belegt eine entsprechende Bewertung der *DGNB*: Für seine hohen energieeffizienten und ökologischen Standards, wie die Verwendung von Holz aus meist heimischen Wäldern und energieoptimierter Fassade sowie einer Bewertung des Betriebs und des gesamten *Lebenszyklus*, wurde das Kongresshaus bereits als weltweit erstes mit einem *DGNB*-Vorzertifikat in Gold ausgezeichnet. Es ist ein erklärtes Ziel der Messe

60,000m² gardens. Together with the adjacent shopping centre, **Skyline Plaza**, the Congress Centre is a highlight in the European quarter. Construction has begun in april 2012. The opening is scheduled for 2014. The existing Congress Centre of Messe Frankfurt from 1997 will be complemented by a reinforced concrete structure which on four event levels offers a hall for 1,000 people, a hall for 600 people and 12 smaller meeting rooms. The Kap Europa is a role model with regard to environmentally and socially responsible construction and operation. This is documented accordingly by an evaluation of the *DGNB*: For its high energy-efficient and environmental standards, such as the use of wood from mostly local forests, energy-optimized facades and the evaluation of the operation and complete life-cycle, the Congress Centre has already been awarded with a Pre-Certificate in Gold as the first congress center ever. It is a stated goal of Messe Frankfurt to create one of the world's most sustainable congress centres. Currently, Messe Frankfurt, the largest German exhibition company, offers 10

The new energy-efficient buildings of the European district and other buildings presented in this book can be visited on guided tours. More information and registration at:
Susanne Petry,
Dipl. Ing. Arch.
Architecture in dialogue
Phone: 0 69-66 57 59 70
E-Mail: petry@architekturimdialog.de

Kap Europa:

The first congress building world wide with a DGNB Pre-Certificate in Gold

Kap Europa:

Energetic Level
| Sustainability demands on the construction and operation of *DGNB*, Pre-Certificate in Gold
| Undercut the *EnEV* 2009 by up to 30%

Use (renewable) energy
| Usage of environment-friendly materials
| High level of daylight and innovative lighting concept with LED usage
| Concrete core *activation* (cooling)
| High quality designed vegetated roof

Kap Europa

3 | Westend

Der ‚MesseTurm':
Frankfurter Wahrzeichen mit LEED-Zertifikat in Silber

Messeturm:

Bauherr / Client
Tishman Speyer Properties, derzeitiger Eigentümer/current owner: GLL Real Estate Partners GmbH

Architekt / Architect
Helmut Jahn –
Büro ‚Murphy/Jahn',
Chicago

**Baujahr /
Year of construction**
1988–1991

Nutzfläche/Useful area
61.700 m²

Energetisches Niveau
| LEED-Zertifikat in Silber 2012 für ‚Existing Building', Bestandsgebäude
| Zertifizierung in Gold für den Innenausbau der neuen Niederlassung der BNY Mellon
| Green Property Management
| Green-Clean-Policy
| LEED konforme Einkaufspolitik und Mieterausbauten
| New Building Automation
| LED-Beleuchtung in der Pyramide

Messeturm

Frankfurt, bezogen auf den Bau und den Betrieb eines der weltweit nachhaltigsten Kongressgebäude zu schaffen. Beim größten deutschen Messeunternehmen können derzeit auf 578.000 m² Grundfläche 10 Hallen, das bereits vorhandene Congress Center und weitere Locations genutzt werden.

Wir folgen der Osloer Straße und gehen in die kleine Grünanlage mit einer Lichtskulptur von Christian Herdeg von 1997. Die angrenzenden Türme **Kastor** und **Pollux** bilden zusammen den Komplex Forum Frankfurt. Am Platz der Einheit biegen wir links in die Friedrich-Ebert-Anlage ab und erreichen so unser nächstes Ziel.

Der fast 257 m hohe **Messeturm** prägt weithin sichtbar das Stadtbild. Der Stahlbetonbau mit 63 Etagen wurde als Entrée für die **Messe Frankfurt** im Stil der Art-Déco-Wolkenkratzer der 1920er bis 1940er Jahre errichtet. Seine Lochfassade aus poliertem Granit verweist auf den traditionellen lokalen Baustoff vergangener Jahrhunderte, den roten Mainsandstein. Das von den Frankfurtern auch ‚Bleistift' genannte Wahrzeichen besitzt die höchste Büroetage Europas. Nach Optimierungen in Technik und Betrieb ist es zudem eines der ersten Hochhäuser des Kontinents mit der Auszeichnung LEED Silber Existing Building. Dabei wurden der Standort, die Gebäudekonzeption

Westend | 3

halls as well as the Congress Center and further event facilities on 578,000 m² of exhibition space. Following the Osloer Straße we enter the small park with a light sculpture by Christian Herdeg from 1997. The adjoining towers **Castor** and **Pollux** make up the complex Forum Frankfurt. At Platz der Einheit, we turn left into Friedrich-Ebert-Anlage and thus reach our next destination.

The almost 257m high **Messeturm** (exhibition tower) widely visible from afar is distinctive in the city. The reinforced concrete construction with 63 floors is an entrée for **Frankfurt's Exhibition Centre** in the style of the Art Deco skyscrapers of the 1920s to 1940s. The perforated facade of polished granite refers to the traditional local building material of past centuries, red Main sandstone. The Landmark,

Kap Europa:

Characteristic, tip
In immediate vicinity of the shoppingcenter Skyline Plaza and connection to public transport.
www.kapeuropa.de

The 'MesseTurm':

The Frankfurt landmark 'MesseTurm' with a Silver LEED Certificate

Messeturm:

Energetic Level
| Silver *LEED* Certificate in 2012 for 'Existing Building'
| Gold Certificate for the interior of the new BNY Mellon branch
| Green Property Management
| Green-Clean-Policy
| Retail policy and tenant residences in accord with *LEED*
| New Building Automation
| LED lights in the pyramid

Characteristic, tip
An extraordinary idea was realised on the 10th floor. The entire area is used as a meeting and conference centre: eight conference rooms, two lounges and a bistro can be used for internal and external events. www.messeturm-services.com

Messeturm

3 | Westend

Messeturm:

Besonderheit, Tipp
Eine außergewöhnliche Idee wurde im 10. Stockwerk realisiert. Die gesamte Fläche dient als Meeting- und Conference-Center: acht Konferenzräume, zwei Lounges und ein Bistro können für interne und externe Veranstaltungen genutzt werden. www.messeturm-services.com

Messehalle 10:

Private Stromerzeugung auf dem Messedach

Dach Messehalle 10:

Bauherr/Client
Bürger aus Frankfurt und Umgebung mit Unterstützung/Citizens with the support of Messe Frankfurt GmbH + Mainova AG

Baujahr/ Year of construction
2009

Nutzfläche/Useful area
3.545 m²

Energetisches Niveau
| Leistung Bauabschnitt 1+2: 490 kWp, Jahresverbrauch von etwa 153 Haushalten

Nutzung (erneuerbarer) Energien
| Solarenergie: *Photovoltaik*

und -substanz sowie die Betriebsmanagementprozesse bewertet.

Direkt neben dem Turm steht seit 1991 die bewegliche Skulptur ‚Hammering Man' des Künstlers Jonathan Borofsky. Links davon liegt die **Festhalle** von 1907 mit ihrer freitragenden Kuppel aus Stahl und Glas zwischen steinernen Ecktürmen. In ihr finden regelmäßig Konzerte und Ausstellungen statt. Geradeaus sehen wir das **Congress Center Messe Frankfurt** mit angeschlossenem Maritim Hotel sowie die Dächer der ersten Messehallen auf dem Gelände der Ludwig-Erhard-Anlage 1.

Ein Vorzeigeprojekt für die Nutzung von Sonnenenergie ist die **Bürgersolaranlage auf dem Dach der Messehalle 10,** die aus den übrigen Bauten auf dem Gelände herausragt. Deshalb errichtete die Messe Frankfurt dort gemeinsam mit der Sonneninitiative e.V. und der Mainova AG eine *Photovoltaik*anlage, deren Montagewannen aus Recyclingkunststoff bestehen. An ihr konnten Bürger und Mitarbeiter der Messe Anteile erwerben. Die Inbetriebnahme des 1. Bauabschnitts erfolgte am 1. Oktober 2009 und vermeidet jährlich etwa 225 t CO_2-Emmissionen. Auf 2.145 m² Fläche produzieren 1.305 polykristalline Solarmodule Strom. Die Maximalleistung beträgt 300 kW. Die Anlage kann

Bürgersolaranlage, Dach/Roof Messehalle 10

also known to locals as 'The Pencil', is the highest office tower in Europe. After optimizations procedures in technology and business, it is also one of the first skyscrapers of the continent to be awarded the Silver in *LEED* 'Existing Building'. The evaluated factors were the location, the design and substance of the building as well as the operational management processes.

Since 1991, the mobile sculpture, 'Hammering Man' by the artist Jonathan Borofsky has been next to the tower. To its left is the **Festhalle** (banquet hall) from 1907, where regular concerts and exhibitions take place. It has a dome of cantilevered steel and glass placed between stone towers. Straight ahead, we see the **Congress Centre** with the adjacent Maritim Hotel and the roofs of the first exhibition halls on the premises of the Ludwig-Erhard-Anlage 1. The **publicly owned solar panels on the roof of Messehalle 10** are a showcase for the use of solar energy. Here, the Messe Frankfurt together with the Sonneninitiative e.V. and Mainova AG, built a *photovoltaic* system, the frames of which are made from recycled plastic. Citizens and employees of the Messe Frankfurt had the opportunity to buy shares of the solar panels. The inauguration of the first construction phase took place on 1st October 2009 and annually avoids about 225 tons of CO_2 emissions. 1,305 solar modules produce electricity on an area of 2,145m². The maximum power produced is 300kW. The system can thus supply about 90 households with electricity. Just 3 months later, the 32.5m solar power plant had been significantly expanded. The 792 modules of the 2nd construction phase now provide further 60 households with electricity and save approximately 142 tons of CO_2 emissions. In 2010 **a *photovoltaic* system went into operation on the roof of the exhibition centre's**

Messehalle 10:

Private power generation on the exhibition centre roof

Roof Messehalle 10:

Energetic Level
| Annual consumption of about 153 households

Use (renewable) energy
| Solar energy: *photovoltaic*

Characteristic, tip

The urban program, 'Frankfurt saves power' helps the Frankfurt residents to reduce their electricity costs by up to 25%. There is also a solar land-map in Internet. It provides interested citizens information on whether the installation of a solar system on their roof is worthwhile and how this can be promoted www.solardach.hessen.de

3 | Westend

Besonderheit, Tipp
Das städtische Programm ‚Frankfurt spart Strom' hilft den Frankfurterinnen und Frankfurtern dabei, ihre Stromkosten um bis zu 25% zu reduzieren. Im Internet existiert zudem ein Solarkataster. Es gibt interessierten Bürgern Auskunft darüber, ob sich die Installation einer Solaranlage auf ihrem Hausdach lohnt und wie diese gefördert werden kann: www.solardach.hessen.de

Systemsporthallen:
Sie verbinden Wirtschaftlichkeit, Ökologie und Flexibilität. 2010 wurden sie mit dem *Passivhaus*-Sonderpreis des Bundesministeriums für Verkehr, Bauwesen und Städtebau ausgezeichnet. Mehrere dieser Neubauten ersetzen inzwischen marode Turnhallen aus den 1960er Jahren. Sie sollen bei insgesamt 27 Projekten zum Einsatz kommen.

so rund 90 Privathaushalte mit Strom versorgen. Nur 3 Monate später wurde das Sonnenkraftwerk in 32,5 m Höhe deutlich erweitert: Die 792 Module des 2. Bauabschnitts versehen nun weitere 60 Haushalte mit Strom und sparen dabei etwa 142 t CO_2-Ausstoß ein. 2010 ging dann auf dem **Dach des Messeparkhauses am Rebstock erstmals eine *Photovoltaik*anlage in Betrieb,** in die Solar-Carports auf einem Parkhaus integriert sind. Und das Engagement geht weiter: Oberbürgermeister Peter Feldmann will die Stadt zum deutschen Solarmeister machen. Laut einer Studie der Universität Frankfurt könnte die Stadt und dreiviertel der umliegenden Kommunen ihren Strombedarf ab 2030 zu 100% aus *erneuerbaren Energien* decken.

Wir gehen nach rechts zur Hamburger Allee und erreichen das **Westend Gate** mit dem Marriott Hotel und Büroflächen. Durch *Photovoltaik*module an der Fassade und die Erneuerung von Klimatisierung und Beleuchtung reduzierte sich der Energieverbrauch bislang um rund 36%.

Wir lassen das Marriott rechts von uns liegen und folgen der Hamburger Allee nach Westen. An der Varrentrappstraße wechseln wir die Straßenseite und gelangen zur Hamburger Allee 43. Hier gilt unser Augenmerk der Einfeld-Turnhalle mit mattierter Glasfassade, die den Hof der **Bonifatiusschule** zur Straße hin schließt. Das Gebäude wurde mit modularen, grau gestrichenen Holzelementen errichtet – als Ergebnis eines von der Stadt Frankfurt im Jahr 2006 ausgeschriebenen Wettbewerbs für ein Turnhallen-Baukastensystem. Der architektonisch ansprechende Prototyp verfügt über einen hohen Vorfertigungsgrad. Das *Passivhaus* wurde anhand von vier ausgewählten Schulstandorten entwickelt.

Wir kehren zur Varrentrappstraße zurück, folgen ihrem gebogenen Verlauf nach Norden und über-

multi-storey garage at the Rebstock; this is the first time that solar carports are integrated into a car park. And the commitment continues: Lord Mayor Peter Feldmann wants to make the city 'Solar Champion' in Germany. According to a study by the University of Frankfurt, the city and three quarters of the surrounding communities could, as of 2030, have their electricity needs met totally by 100% *renewable energy*.

We go right to the Hamburger Allee and arrive at the **Westend Gate** with the Marriott hotel and office premises. Here, solar facade modules were installed, the air conditioning system was renewed and the lighting optimised. Thus, energy consumption was reduced so far by 36%.

We leave the Marriott to the right and follow the Hamburger Allee westwards. At the Varrentrappstraße we cross the road and go to Hamburger Allee 43. Here we see the Einfeld-Gymnasium with its frosted glass front, which has been built on the boundaries of the **St. Boniface School** yard. It was erected with modular, grey-painted wooden elements – as a result of a competition organized by the City of Frankfurt in 2006, for a modular gymnasium system. The architecturally attractive prototype has a high degree of prefabrication.

System gymnasiums:

They combine economy, ecology and flexibility. In 2010, they were awarded the *Passive House* special prize from the Federal Ministry of Transport, Building and Urban Development. Several of these buildings now replace dilapidated gyms from the 1960s. This method should be adopted for a total of 27 projects.

Bonifatiusschule /St. Boniface School

3 | Westend

Kulturcampus:

Modellquartier des 21. Jahrhunderts

Kulturcampus:

Bauherr / Client
ABG Frankfurt Holding GmbH

Architekt / Architect
1. Bauabschnitt: happarchitecture, Stefan Forster Architekten GmbH, Karl Dudler Architekt – Frankfurt am Main

Baujahr/Year of constr.
2011–2021

Areal/Entire area
16,5 ha

Energetisches Niveau
| *Passivhäuser*

Nutzung (erneuerbarer) Energien
Es soll ein Modellquartier geschaffen werden, das CO_2-neutral, energieeffizient und nachhaltig ist sowie die Wärme des Abwassers nutzt.

Besonderheit, Tipp
Geplant: Künstler geben auf dem Campus Einblicke in ihre Arbeit, gleichzeitig unterrichtet die Stadt über das, was gemeinsam mit privaten Partnern in den kommenden Jahren entstehen wird. Dabei sollen die Frankfurter involviert sein – ebenso wie durch die Homepage: www.kulturcampusfrankfurt.de

queren den **Theodor-W.-Adorno-Platz**. Durch die Robert-Mayer-Straße kommen wir zur Senckenberganlage. Das Gebiet, der ehemalige ‚Uni-Campus Bockenheim' der Johann-Wolfgang-Goethe-Universität, wird nachhaltig umgestaltet. Der **Kulturcampus** entsteht auf dem 16,5 ha großen Areal, das die Stadtteile **Bockenheim** und **Westend** künftig miteinander verbindet. In dem Viertel sollen Produktionsstätten und Unterrichtsorte für Musiker, Schauspieler und Tänzer sowie bis zu 1.500 neue Wohnungen, Büros und Gastronomiebetriebe entstehen. Das zentrale Kulturquartier bietet Platz für die Musikhochschule, das Ensemble Modern, die Theaterakademie, die Forsythe Company, das Hindemith-Institut, das LAB Frankfurt und zahlreiche freie Produktionsgruppen, die künftig vor allem das Studierendenhaus nutzen wollen. Möglich wird dies durch die Übertragung des Geländes von dem Land Hessen an die ABG, dem Wohnungs- und Immobilienkonzern der Stadt Frankfurt. Die Goethe-Universität zieht auf den Campus Westend und Riedberg. Als erste Baumaßnahme errichtet die ABG auf dem 9.000 m^2 großen Eckgrundstück Sophienstraße/Gräfstraße im Norden eine siebenstöckige Bebauung mit 200 Wohnungen, Tiefgarage sowie Supermarkt. Der Kulturcampus soll die sozialen, wirtschaftlichen und kulturellen Strukturen der gesamten Stadt vitalisieren. Leitlinien der Planungen sind eine nachhaltige Wohnstruktur, kommunikationsfördernde Architektur und kreative Vernetzung. Bei dem ambitionierten Modellprojekt soll auch die Beziehung von Kultur und Natur in zeitgemäßer Form deutlich und die angestrebte Energiewende in weiteren Zusammenhängen gedacht werden, also kein isoliertes Leuchtturm-Projekt entstehen.

Wir laufen die Senckenberganlage weiter und erreichen links das 1907 in der Tradition des

Westend | 3

Plan Kulturcampus

Modell Kulturcampus

Kulturcampus:

Model living in the 21st Century

Kulturcampus:

Energetic Level
| *Passive Houses*

Use (renewable) energy
It is the aim to create a model estate which is CO_2 neutral and energy-efficient and uses the heat from waste water.

Characteristic, tip
Planned: On campus artists give insight into their work; at the same time the city informs its citizens about what is possible in collaboration with private partners in the coming years. The Frankfurters should be involved in this – as well as through the website: www.kulturcampusfrankfurt.de

We return to Varrentrappstraße, follow the curved road and cross the **Theodor-W.-Adorno-Platz**. Along the Robert-Mayer-Straße we come to Senckenberganlage. The area of the former campus Bockenheim of the 'Johann Wolfgang Goethe' University is being sustainably transformed.

The **Kulturcampus** is being built on the 16.5 hectare area, which will connect the city and districts **Bockenheim** and **Westend** with each other. Here, manufacturing and educational facilities for musicians, actors and dancers, as well as up to 1,500 new homes, offices and restaurants are in development. The central cultural district has room for the Academy of Music, Ensemble Modern, and Theatre Academy, the Forsythe Company, the Hindemith Institute, the Frankfurt LAB and many independent

3 | Westend

KfW Ostarkade:
Ressourcenschonender, vorbildlicher Neubau

KfW Ostarkade:

Bauherr / Client
KfW Bankengruppe

Architekt / Architect
RKW Rhode Kellermann Wawrowsky GmbH + Co. KG Architektur + Städtebau, Düsseldorf

Baujahr/
Year of construction
2000–2002

Nutzfläche/Useful area
14.986 m²

Energetisches Niveau
| Auszeichnung als ‚Green Building Frankfurt' in 2009

Nutzung (erneuerbarer) Energien
| Solarthermie für Warmwasser und Heizung in den Mietwohnungen
| Holzpelletkessel für Heizung + Gaskessel zur Spitzenlastabdeckung
| Natürliche Lüftung und Belichtung
| Nutzung von Regenwasser
| Bezug von Ökostrom

barocken Schlossbaus errichtete Gebäude für die ‚Senckenbergische naturforschende Gesellschaft'. Dort befindet sich auch das **Senckenberg Museum**, ein Naturkundemuseum, das die Themen Biodiversität, Evolution und Erdgeschichte anschaulich macht. Anschließend gehen wir zur Kreuzung Bockenheimer Landstraße, die wir überqueren. Dabei sehen wir links hinunter die Bockenheimer Warte, einen spätgotischen Wehrturm von 1434/35, und rechts auf der Ecke die **Gebäude der KfW Bankengruppe**. Ihr neuester Bürobau in Frankfurt, die ‚**Westarkade**', besitzt einen der höchsten Ökostandards weltweit: Dank der zweischichtigen Druckringfassade, der Nutzung eines Erdwärmetauschers, der Verwendung der Abwärme aus dem Rechenzentrum und weiterer energieeffizienter Gebäudetechnik beträgt der jährliche

KfW Westarkade

production groups who would especially like to make use of the students' centre. This is possible due to the transfer of the land from the state of Hessen to the ABG, the housing and real estate Company belonging to the city of Frankfurt. The Goethe University will move to the Campus Westend and Riedberg. As an initial measure the ABG will develop a seven-storey building with 200 apartments, an underground car park and a supermarket on the 9,000m^2 corner plot at Sophienstraße/Gräfstraße in the north.

The cultural campus is intended to revitalize the social, economic and cultural structures of the entire city. Guidelines for planning are a sustainable residential structure, pro-communication architecture and creative networking. This ambitious pilot project also wants to emphasise the relationship between nature and culture in a contemporary form and take into consideration the desired energy turnaround in further contexts. Thus, it is not intended to be an isolated project.

We walk along the Senckenberganlage and see on the left the building of the Senckenberg natural research society; this was built in 1907 in traditional baroque style. The **Senckenberg Museum** is also located here; a natural history museum that vividly shows topics such as biodiversity, evolution and geological history. Then we go to the junction with Bockenheimer Landstrasse and cross the road. We see on the left the late Gothic Bockenheimer look-out tower from 1434/35 and on the right corner the **buildings of the KfW banking group**. Their newest office building in Frankfurt, named **'Westarkade'**, has one of the highest ecological standards in the world: due to the two-layer pressure ring facade, the use of a geothermal heat exchanger, the reuse of waste heat from the data centre as well as

KfW Ostarkade:

Resource-saving, commendable new building

KfW Ostarkade:

Energetic Level
| Awarded as *'Green Building Frankfurt'* in 2009

Use (renewable) energy
| Solar energy for hot water and heating in rental apartments
| Wooden pellet boilers for heating and gas boiler to cover peak loads
| Natural ventilation and lighting
| Use of rainwater
| Purchase of green electricity

Characteristic, tip
Innovative lighting solution for workplaces:
| Flush ceiling windows which supply light to a room depth of 5.5m
| External blinds with a daylight divertable upper part (glare-free light closed state)
| Multifunctional canopies for daylight deflection, lighting, presence/light sensors, room acoustics and, where necessary, cooling

3 | Westend

KfW Ostarkade:

Besonderheit, Tipp
Innovative Lichtlösung für Arbeitsplätze:
- Deckenbündige Fenster zur Lichtversorgung bis 5,5 m Raumtiefe
- Außenliegende Jalousien mit Tageslicht umlenkendem oberen Teil (blendfreies Licht in heruntergefahrenem Zustand)
- Multifunktionales Deckensegel für Tageslichtumlenkung, Beleuchtung, Präsenz-/Lichtsensoren, Raumakustik und gegebenenfalls Raumkühlung

KfW Haupthaus:

Mit eigenem, guten Sanierungsbeispiel voran gehen

KfW Haupthaus:

Bauherr / Client
KfW Bankengruppe

Architekt / Architect
RKW Rhode Kellermann Wawrowsky GmbH + Co. KG Architektur + Städtebau, Düsseldorf

**Baujahr /
Year of construction**
2004–2006

Nutzfläche/Useful area
21.446 m²

KfW Ostarkade

Primärenergiebedarf maximal 100 kWh/m². Das ressourceneffiziente Gebäude erhielt 2011 die Auszeichnung ‚Best Tall Building in the World'. Wir überqueren nun die Zeppelinallee und wandern unter den Arkaden der KfW entlang. Hinter einem Wasserbecken erreichen wir links unser nächstes Ziel. Die **KfW Ostarkade** an der **Palmengartenstraße** besteht – den gründerzeitlichen Charakter des Frankfurter Westends aufgreifend – aus mehreren Gebäudevolumen, die durch eine einheitliche Fassade zusammengefasst werden. Kernstück des Stahlbetonbaus ist das 15 m hohe Atrium mit einem tonnenförmigen Glasdach: Es versorgt das Innere mit Licht und nutzt die Auftriebskraft von warmer Luft, um das Gebäude bei Bedarf natürlich zu belüften und bei ausreichend niedriger Außenlufttemperatur auch zu kühlen. Der Hochbau verfügt über fünf Büro- und zwei abschließende Wohnetagen. Sein Energiekonzept sowie das konsequente Controlling während der Planungs-, Bau- und Betriebsphasen stellen einen Primärenergiebedarf von rund 90 kWh/(m²a) sicher.

Wir biegen links in die Palmengartenstraße ein. An ihrem Ende weitet sie sich zu einem Platz, von dessen rechter Seite wir einen guten Blick auf einen weiteren energieeffizienten Bau haben. Die Revitalisierung des in den 1960er Jahren

KfW Haupthaus

KfW Haupthaus:
An example of successful refurbishment

other energy-efficient techniques, the annual primary energy demand is a maximum of 100 kWh/m². In 2011 the resource-efficient building received an award for 'Best Tall Building in the World'.

We cross the Zeppelinallee and walk under the arcades along the KfW. Behind a fountain, we reach our next destination.

The **KfW Ostarkade** at **Palmengartenstraße**, which follows Frankfurt's Westend Wilhelminian character, is made up of multiple buildings, which are consolidated by a single facade. The centrepiece of the reinforced concrete construction is the 15m high atrium with a barrel-shaped glass roof. It supplies the interior with light and uses the buoyancy of warm air to ventilate the building when necessary and to cool if the external air temperature is sufficiently low. The building has five office floors and two separate residential floors at the top. The building's energy concept and consistent controlling during the planning, construction and operation phases ensures a primary energy requirement of about 90kWh/(m²a).

We turn left into Palmengartenstraße. At its end, it opens out to a plaza from the right of which we have a good view of another energy-efficient construction.

3 | Westend

KfW Haupthaus:
Energetisches Niveau
| Auszeichnung als ‚Green Building Frankfurt' in 2009

Nutzung (erneuerbarer) Energien
| Solarthermie für Warmwasser und Heizung
| Gaskessel für Heizung
| Natürliche Lüftung und Belichtung
| Nutzung von Regenwasser
| Bezug von Ökostrom

Besonderheit, Tipp
Einen wichtigen Beitrag zur Ressourcenschonung leistet das ambitionierte Wasserkonzept: Die im gesamten Gebäude installierten Vakuumtoiletten benötigen pro Spülgang etwa 80% weniger Wasser als herkömmliche Toiletten. Das Abwasser aus den Toiletten wird der Kanalisation zugeführt. Das *Grau-* und Regenwasser werden sinnvoll weiter verwendet, etwa für die Toilettenspülung.

Der im Jahr 1871 eröffnete und durch Heinrich Siesmayer angelegte **Palmengarten** entsprang wie viele andere Frankfurter Institutionen und Sehenswürdigkeiten privater bürgerlicher Initiative.

erbauten **Haupthauses der KfW**, die größte deutsche Umwelt- und Klimabank, ist eine architektonische Aufwertung und reduziert den ursprünglichen Primärenergiebedarf um fast 60%. Wichtigster Teil ist die neue Fassade. Sie umschließt das Gebäude mit einer funktionalen Hülle, die auf äußere Bedingungen, wie Temperatur oder Sonneneinstrahlung, reagieren kann. Ihre Verglasung lässt viel Licht und wenig Wärme in die Räume. Die senkrecht verstellbaren Sonnenschutzelemente geben dem barrierefreien Bau eine lebendige Anmutung.

Hinter dem jetzigen **Nebeneingang des Palmengartens** sehen wir auch sein **Gesellschaftshaus**. Es ist denkmalgerecht instand gesetzt und modernisiert worden. Der Entwurf von David Chipperfield Architects vereinigt die historische Bausubstanz mit einem neuen Westflügel, der das Erbe des Neuen Frankfurt interpretiert. Der Festsaal mit Fenstern zum Palmenhaus erstrahlt seit 2012 wieder im Stil der Neorenaissance. Das Haus bietet Veranstaltungen mit bis zu 1.300 Personen Platz.

Wir verlassen den Platz mit Blick auf das historische Galeriehaus rechts, folgen der Bockenheimer Landstraße nach links und biegen links in die Siesmayerstraße ab. Bei Nr. 12 entdecken wir die Villa Bonn aus dem Jahr 1897. Das großbürgerliche Palais wurde von dem Berliner Hofbaumeister Ernst Eberhart von Ihne erbaut. Schräg gegenüber befindet sich das ehemalige amerikanische Generalkonsulat. Das 2007/08 sanierte Bürogebäude ist ein Meisterstück der Klassischen Moderne. Der Nachkriegsbau aus Beton, Stahl und Glas entstand nach Plänen des Architekturbüros SOM aus Chicago.

Am **Grüneburgweg**, der Grenze Westend Süd zu Westend Nord, liegt der **Haupteingang des Palmengartens**, in dem wir verschiedenste thematische Gärten und Gewächshäuser mit

The revitalization of the **main building of KfW** from the 1960s, the largest German environmental and climate bank, has been architecturally enhanced and its original primary energy consumption is now reduced by almost 60%. The most important part is the new facade. It surrounds the building with a functional shell which is responsive to external conditions, such as temperature or sunlight. Its glazing allows plenty of light and little heat into the rooms. The vertically adjustable sun protection elements give the barrier free building a vibrant appearance.

Behind the current **side entrance of the Palmengarten** (botanical garden), we also see its **events building**. It has been repaired and modernised according to the guidelines for listed buildings. The design by David Chipperfield Architects complements the historical architecture with a new west wing, which reflects the heritage of a New Frankfurt. Since 2012, the ballroom, with its windows overlooking the palm trees building, radiates anew in Neo-Renaissance style and can host events for up to 1,300 people.

We leave the plaza with a view of the historic gallery building on the right, follow the Bockenheimer Landstraße to the left and turn left into the Siesmayerstraße. At No. 12, we discover the Villa Bonn from 1897. The bourgeois palace was built by the Berlin court architect Ernst Eberhart von Ihne. Diagonally opposite is the former U.S. Consulate. The 2007/08 refurbished office building is a masterpiece of classical modernism. The post-war building of concrete, steel and glass was designed by the architects company SOM from Chicago.

On **Grüneburgweg**, the border between Westend South and Westend North is the

KfW Haupthaus:

Energetic Level
| Awarded as *'Green Building Frankfurt'* in 2009

Use (renewable) energy
| Solar energy for hot water and heating
| Gas boiler for heating
| Natural ventilation and lighting
| Use of rainwater
| Purchase of green electricity

Characteristic, tip
The ambitious water concept makes an important contribution to the conservation of resources: The vacuum toilets installed throughout the building need per flush cycle about 80% less water than conventional toilets. The wastewater from the toilets is runs into the sewage system. The *grey water* and rainwater are used more meaningfully, such as for flushing the toilet.

The Palmengarten which opened in 1871 was created by Heinrich Siesmayer as the result of a private civil initiative.

Haupteingang/Main entrance Palmengarten

Pflanzen aus allen Erdteilen erkunden können. Im Tropicarium betreibt die Mainova ein **Blockheizkraftwerk** mit einem Gesamtwirkungsgrad von rund 87%. Der Kessel wird mit Erdgas befeuert. Die erzeugte Wärme kommt den Palmen und anderen tropischen Pflanzen ganzjährig zu Gute. Außerdem versorgt die ferngesteuerte Anlage das benachbarte Biologische Institut der Goethe-Universität mit Wärme. Der erzeugte Strom wird ins Netz eingespeist.

Wenn wir der Siesmayerstraße nach Norden folgen, schließt sich der **Botanische Garten** an. In ihm sind über 5.000 Arten von Freilandpflanzen zu sehen, die hauptsächlich zur heimischen, mitteleuropäischen Flora gehören. Ebenfalls direkt benachbart liegt der weitläufige **Grüneburgpark**. Östlich von ihm, parallel zur Fürstenbergerstraße, können wir die 1930 von Hans Poelzig errichtete ehemalige Konzernzentrale der IG Farben entdecken. Sie ist eines der bedeutendsten Bauwerke des 20. Jahrhunderts und war Hauptsitz der US-amerikanischen Streitkräfte in Europa. Seit 2001 befindet sich hier der ‚**Uni-Campus Westend**' der Goethe-Universität. Seit 2009 nimmt sie an ‚ÖKOPROFIT' teil, einer Aktion der Stadt Frankfurt. Ziel ist, durch die Erarbeitung und Umsetzung praxisnaher betriebsspezifischer Maßnahmen weniger Energie und Rohstoffe zu verbrauchen.

main entrance of the Palmengarten, where we can explore several thematic gardens and greenhouses with plants from around the world. In the Tropicarium the Mainova AG operates a *CHP* with an overall efficiency of about 87%. The boiler is fired with natural gas. The heat produced is of benefit for the palm trees and other tropical plants all year round. Furthermore, the remote controlled system supplies the neighbouring Biological Institute of the Goethe University with heat. The electricity thus generated is fed into the grid.

If we follow the Siesmayerstraße to the north we come to the **Botanical Garden**. In it more than 5,000 types of outdoor plants can be seen that belong mainly to the domestic, Central European flora. Directly adjacent to it is the spacious **Grüneburgpark**. East of it, parallel to Fürstenbergerstraße, we discover the former headquarters of IG Farben from 1930, built by Hans Poelzig. It is one of the most important buildings of the 20th Century and was the headquarters of the U.S. Armed Forces in Europe. Since 2001 the **'Uni-Campus Westend'** of the Goethe University is located here. Since 2009, the university participates in 'ÖKOPROFIT', a project of the City of Frankfurt. The goal is to consume less energy and fewer resources through the development and implementation of practical plant-specific measures.

4 | Westend – Innenstadt

Route Westend Süd – Innenstadt – Nordend

Die Landschaft des **Westends** war seit Ende des 14. Jahrhunderts Teil der Frankfurter Gemarkung innerhalb der Landwehr, einem Grenzsicherungswerk vor den Stadtmauern. Straßennamen wie der **Kettenhofweg** erinnern heute noch an die damaligen Gutshöfe. Im 19. Jahrhundert entstanden hier und um die Innenstadt viele klassizistische Villen mit Gärten und großzügige Wohnhäuser. Ab Anfang des 20. Jahrhunderts sollte der **Alleenring** diese Bebauungen eingrenzen und sie gleichzeitig miteinander verbinden.

Unsere Erkundungstour starten wir an der U-Bahn-Station ‚Westend'. In der Feuerbachstraße Nr. 40 sehen wir gleich – links hinter einer Info-Box – unser erstes Ziel.

Beim **Projekt Vero** werden insgesamt 118 Wohnungen und ein Bürohaus errichtet. Die Wohnungen verteilen sich auf einen Riegelbau und **sechs Stadtvillen**. Sie befinden sich in einem der begehrtesten Frankfurter Viertel und setzen bei der Energieversorgung auf *erneuerbare Energien* sowie auf die höchste *DGNB*-Zertifizierung. Bereits in der Planung wurden Ökologie, also Energieverbrauch und Schadstoffausstoß, Ökonomie, die Wirtschaftlichkeit im *Lebenszyklus*,

Westend:

Es setzt sich aus den Stadtteilen Westend Süd und Westend Nord zusammen und gilt als gehobenes, bürgerliches Viertel mit teuren Immobilien. Das Westend, das Bahnhofsviertel, das Nord- und Ostend zeichnen sich durch Gründerzeitarchitektur aus. Gemeinsam bilden sie die verdichteten Bezirke rund um die Frankfurter Innenstadt.

Projekt ‚VERO':

Die Stadtvillen gehören zu den ersten bundesweiten Wohngebäuden mit DGNB-Zertifikat in Gold

Projekt Vero:

Bauherr / Client
PATRIZIA Projektentwicklung GmbH, F40 GmbH

Architekt / Architect
lauber + zottmann GmbH, München

Baujahr / Year of construction
2011–2013

Projekt Vero, Stadtvillen/Town houses

Westend – City Centre | 4

Projekt Vero, Stadtvillen/Town houses

Tour Southern Westend – City Centre – Nordend

The **Westend** has been part of the Frankfurt district within the Landwehr (border security outside the city walls) since the end of the 14th Century. Street names like the **Kettenhofweg** remind us of the former estates. In the 19th Century many classical villas with gardens and spacious residences were built around the city centre. From the beginning of the 20th Century the **Alleenring** forms a border round these estates and at the same time interconnects them.

We start our exploration tour at the underground station 'Westend'. At Feuerbachstraße No. 40 we see our first goal straight away, behind and to the left of an information box.
As part of the **project Vero** a total of 118 apartments and an office building were built. The apartments are of a timber framed construction and **six town houses**. They are situated in one of the most sought-after districts of Frankfurt, and using *renewable energy* for the energy supply, so the highest *DGNB* certification was of the

Westend:

The combined suburbs Westend South and Westend North are an exclusive part of the city with desirable but expensive properties. Much of the Westend, the area around the station and the Northend and Eastend were constructed at the end of the 19th/beginning of the 20th Century forming a tight circle round Frankfurt's inner city.

Project 'VERO':

The town villas are amongst the first nationwide residential buildings with DGNB Certificate in Gold

4 | Westend – Innenstadt

Projekt Vero:

Energetisches Niveau
DGNB-Vorzertifikat in Gold für Wohngebäude

Nutzung (erneuerbarer) Energien
| Solarkollektoren für Warmwasser
| Luft/Wasser-*Wärmepumpe* für Heizung im Winter und Kühlung im Sommer

---

Großbürgerliche Gründerzeitbauten prägen das Westend – ergänzt um Gebäude der Nachkriegszeit, die oft wenig Rücksicht auf die vorhandenen Strukturen nahmen. 1970 wurde für das Gebiet eine ‚Veränderungssperre' veröffentlicht.

Prozess- und Standortqualitäten sowie funktionale und technische Aspekte berücksichtigt – ebenso alle Faktoren, die das Wohlbefinden der Nutzer beeinflussen. Die Räume der Stadtvillen können individuell eingeteilt werden. Da nur die Gebäudehülle und der Treppenhauskern tragende Elemente sind, stellt der Ein- oder Rückbau von Wänden oder das Herstellen von Barrierefreiheit kein Problem dar. Zudem haben die Bewohner die Möglichkeit, ihre Haus- und Sicherheitstechnik via Smartphone oder Tabletcomputer zu steuern. Das ökologische Konzept verbindet niedrige Betriebskosten mit einer hellen und eleganten Architektur. Sie greift die stadtgestalterisch typische Villenstruktur des Westends auf. Moderne Fassaden mit hohen Glaselementen und wertigen Materialien, großzügige Terrassen und eine lichte Raumhöhe bis zu 3,29 m gehören ebenso dazu wie der parkähnliche, über 1.700 m² große Garten.

Wir folgen der Feuerbachstraße an der Bettinaschule vorbei. Seit 1999 besitzt die Schule eine *Photovoltaik*anlage, die hilft, jährlich 0,6 t CO_2 zu vermeiden.

Wir biegen links in den Kettenhofweg ein und laufen weiter mit Sicht auf die Skyline durch das überwiegend zum Wohnen genutzte Gebiet.

An der Kreuzung zur Ulmenstraße fällt uns auf der rechten Ecke das **Livingston'sche Stallgebäude** aus den 1880er Jahren auf. Der Pferdestall mit Remise und Kutscherwohnung wurde für den aus Amerika zurückgekehrten Marks John Livingston errichtet. Die in rotem Sandstein ausgeführte Dreiflügelanlage ziert eine doppelte Torarkade sowie ein schmuckreicher Mittelrisalit. Im Inneren wurden die Kutschen mit einem Aufzugsystem vom 1. Stock herauf- und heruntertransportiert. Wir lassen das Gebäude von Christian Ludwig Schmidt mit einer Atlas-Figur an der Fassadenecke rechts von uns und

Westend – City Centre | 4

utmost importance. As early as in the planning phase all the factors that affect the residents' well-being were taken into consideration; ecology (energy consumption and pollutant emissions), economics (the *lifecycle* cost effectiveness), process and site quality as well as functional and technical aspects. The rooms of the town houses can be individually sized. Only the building outer casing and the staircase core are supporting elements. It is no problem to remove or add a wall or to achieve barrier- free accessibility. Also the residents are able to control their home and security technology via smartphone or tablet computer. The ecological concept combines low operating costs with a light and elegant architecture. The typical design of city villas in the Westend is well represented here. Modern facades with glass elements and high quality materials, spacious terraces and a clear room height of up to 3.29m are just as important as the park-like garden with over 1,700m².

We follow the Feuerbachstraße past the Bettinaschule. Since 1999 the school has had a *photovoltaic* system, which helps to prevent the emission of 0.6 tons of CO_2 annually.

We turn left into the Kettenhofweg and continue further with a view of the skyline through the predominantly residential area.

Project Vero:

Energetic Level
DGNB Pre-Certificate in Gold for residences

Use (renewable) energy
| Solar panels for warm water
| Air/water *heat pump* for heating in winter and cooling in summer

---

The Westend is characterised by upper-class Wilhelminian style buildings – with buildings of the post war period in between, which often took little account of the existing structures. In 1970, the area had a 'development freeze' imposed upon it.

4 | Westend – Innenstadt

Der ‚OpernTurm':
Als eine der ersten Bürohochhaus-Neubauten LEED Gold-Zertifikat

Opernturm:

Bauherr/Client
Opernplatz Property Holdings GmbH & Co. KG

Architekt/Architect
Prof. Christoph Mäckler Architekten, Frankfurt am Main

**Baujahr/
Year of construction**
2006–2009

Nutzfläche/Useful area
66.000 m²

Energetisches Niveau
| LEED-Zertifikat in Gold 2009 für Bürohochhaus, Neubau
| Unterbieten der geforderten Werte der EnEV 2007 um 23%

Nutzung (erneuerbarer) Energien
| Anschluss an das Fernwärmenetz
| Einsatz innovativer und umweltfreundlicher Gebäudetechnik
| Zusätzliche ökologische Akzente setzen die natürliche Lüftung und Beleuchtung

entdecken im Kettenhofweg 29 einen anderen Entwurf des Architekten: die spätklassizistische **Villa Cronhardt**. Ihr markanter Rundbau entstand 1872. An der Fassade bemerken wir Lünetten, ornamentierte Fensterstürze sowie eine Pilastergliederung in der Eckabrundung. Wenige Meter weiter erreichen wir das mit hellem Naturstein verkleidete ‚**mainBuilding**'. Hier halten wir uns rechts, dann links und passieren so die weiträumige Piazza des siebengeschossigen Bürokomplexes von 2005. Seine Innenräume verfügen über viel Tageslicht sowie eine intelligente Gebäudetechnik mit *Wärmerückgewinnung.* Eine denkmalgeschützte Villa schließt den Hof zur Taunusanlage ab. Dort wenden wir uns links dem **Opernturm** zu, dessen Bau zuletzt versiegelte 5.500 m² als Grünfläche an den dahinter liegenden **Rothschildpark** zurückgab. Er ist in seiner ursprünglichen Gestalt rekonstruiert, saniert und neu bepflanzt worden.

Der 170 m hohe **Opernturm** in der Bockenheimer Landstraße 2–4 ergänzt mit seiner siebengeschossigen Blockrandbebauung das großstädtische Ensemble am **Opernplatz** zu einem

Opernturm

Westend – City Centre | 4

At the intersection with Ulmenstraße we see on the right corner the **Livingston'sche stable building** from the 1880s. The stables and coachhouse with carriage house were built for Marks John Livingston return from America. The three wings in red sandstone have a double arched gateway and a decorative central column. Inside, the carriages were transported by an elevator system up to the first floor and down again. We leave the building of Christian Ludwig Schmidt with an Atlas figure on the facade and discover at No. 29 Kettenhofweg another construction by the same architect: the late classical **Villa Cronhardt**. Its distinctive rotunda was built in 1872. On the facade, we notice lunettes, ornamental architraves and a pilaster in the alcove. A few meters further we see the **'main Building'** with pale stone cladding. Here we keep right, then go to the left passing the spacious plaza of the seven-storey office complex built in 2005. Its interiors have plenty of natural light as well as intelligent building technology with a *heat recovery* system. A listed villa closes the courtyard to the Taunusanlage. Here we turn left towards the **Opernturm,** the construction of which sealed the return of 5,500m² green space, to the **Rothschildpark** beyond. The area has been reconstructed in its original form, restored and replanted.

The 170 meter high **Opernturm** in the Bockenheimer Landstrasse 2–4 with its seven-storey perimeter block building complements the metropolitan ensemble at the **Opernplatz**. With the stone facade covering over 50% of the building it takes up the uniform yellow-beige stone cladding of the surrounding buildings. Compared to an all-glass facade it saves 20% of the energy required to cool an office floor. Vertical projections between the window bays also ensure constructive shading and in

Opernturm

The ‚OpernTurm':

One of the first office building gaining a LEED Certificate in Gold

Opernturm:

Energetic Level
| *LEED* Certificate in Gold 2009 for office building
| Undercut the required values of *EnEV* 2007 by 23%

Use (renewable) energy
| Connection to the *district heating* network
| Use of innovative and environment-friendly building techniques
| Natural ventilation and lighting place particular emphasis on additional ecological touches.

4 | Westend – Innenstadt

Opernturm:

Besonderheit, Tipp
Der gesamte Bauschutt wurde wiederverwertet und der Einsatz von receltem Material, wie etwa Aluminium, unterstützt. Dies verringert die *graue Energie* und verbessert die *Ökobilanz* des Gebäudes. Zu diesem Zweck wurden auch die Transportwege so gering wie möglich gehalten.

Alte Oper:

Moderner Veranstaltungsort in historischem Gewand

Alte Oper:

Bauherr/Client
Stadt und Bürger Frankfurts/City and citizens of Frankfurt

Architekt/Architect
Original design: Richard Lucae; Wiederaufbau/Reconstruction: Helmut Braun und Martin Schlockermann

Baujahr/Year of constr.
1880: Opernhaus, Neubau/First built as opera house;
1981: Konzert- und Kongresshaus, Wiederaufbau/Reconstructed as concert and congress hall

Nutzfläche/Useful area
7.750 m²

geschlossenen Platzraum. Die einheitliche gelbbeige Steinverkleidung der umliegenden Bauten greift er mit seiner Natursteinfassade auf. Diese ist zu über 50% geschlossen und spart so im Vergleich zu einer Ganzglasfassade 20% Energie für die Kühlung einer Büroetage ein. Vertikale Vorsprünge zwischen den Fensterachsen sorgen zudem für eine konstruktive Verschattung und reduzieren in Kombination mit einer hocheffizienten Verglasung den Solareintrag. Der Einsatz moderner Hybrid-Heiz-/Kühldecken drosselt den Energiebedarf dann um 30% gegenüber konventionellen Kühldecken.

Wir überqueren die Hauptverkehrsstraße zum Opernplatz mit dem 1983 von Edwin Hüller aus Granit geschaffenen Lucae-Brunnen.

Links, hinter der markanten spätklassizistischen Fassade des ehemaligen Frankfurter Opernhauses, das ursprünglich 1880 und 1981 als Konzert- und Kongresshaus wieder aufgebaut wurde, verbergen sich zwei der international renommiertesten Konzertsäle Deutschlands. Das Programmangebot reicht von Klassik und Jazz bis zu Musicals und Shows. Zudem ist die **Alte Oper Frankfurt** ein außergewöhnlicher und beliebter Kongress- und Veranstaltungsort. Im Café Rosso und im Restaurant Opéra verwöhnt Sie Gerd Käfer und sein Team. Heute erinnern

Alte Oper

Westend – City Centre | 4

Alte Oper

Opernturm:

Characteristic, tip
The entire construction waste was recycled and the use of recycled material, such as aluminium supported. This reduced the *embodied/grey energy* and improved the environmental performance of the building. To this purpose, the transport routes were minimised.

combination with highly efficient glazing reduce the solar input. The use of a modern hybrid heating/cooling system throttles the energy requirement by 30% compared to conventional cooling systems.

We cross the main road to the Opernplatz with the granite Lucae Fountain created by Edwin Hüller in 1983.

Behind the distinctive late classical facade of the **former Frankfurt opera house** are two of the most renowned concert halls in Germany. The house was originally built in 1880 and rebuilt in 1981 as a concert and congress venue. The program ranges from classical and jazz to musicals and shows. In addition, the Alte Oper Frankfurt is an exceptional and popular conference and events location. In the café Rosso and restaurant Opéra, Gerd Käfer and his team take good care of you. Today, only the old foyer with the restaurant and the vestibule resemble the original interior design: After the 2nd World War, 'Germany's most beautiful ruin' was rebuilt with a modern core within a historic casing. Following this example, since 2009 the Alte Oper participates

Alte Oper:

Modern events in historical setting

Alte Oper:

Energetic Level
| 'ÖKOPROFIT Betrieb Frankfurt am Main' 2009/2010

Use (renewable) energy
| Purchase of green electricity and *district heating*
| Air conditioning with *heat recovery*
| Energy-efficient building technology

4 | Westend – Innenstadt

Alte Oper:

Energetisches Niveau
| ‚ÖKOPROFIT Betrieb Frankfurt am Main' 2009/2010

Nutzung (erneuerbarer) Energien
| Bezug von Ökostrom und *Fernwärme*
| Klimaanlage mit *Wärmerückgewinnung*
| Energieeffiziente Gebäudetechnik

Besonderheit, Tipp
Ab 12 Personen sind Führungen in der Alten Oper möglich. Der Preis dafür beträgt 7 € pro Person oder pauschal 84 € bei einer geringeren Teilnehmeranzahl.

Ansprechpartner:
Michael Dückers
Tel.: 01578 5521-843
9.00 – 15.00 Uhr
E-Mail: fuehrungen@alteoper.de
www.alteoper.de

Beliebt ist das *Fressgass'*-Fest im Juni und der Rheingauer Weinmarkt im August.

---

nur das alte Foyer mit dem Restaurant und das Vestibül an die ursprüngliche Raumausstattung: Nach dem 2. Weltkrieg wurde die „schönste Ruine Deutschlands" mit einem modernen Kern innerhalb einer historischen Hülle wieder aufgebaut. Diesem Ansatz folgend nimmt die Alte Oper seit 2009 an ‚ÖKOPROFIT', einer Aktion der Stadt Frankfurt für kleine und mittlere Unternehmen zum Einstieg ins Umweltmanagement, teil. Ziel ist, durch die Erarbeitung und Umsetzung praxisnaher betriebsspezifischer Maßnahmen weniger Energie und Rohstoffe zu verbrauchen. Dies führt zu geringeren Betriebskosten und entlastet die Umwelt um jährlich insgesamt über 21.000 t CO_2. Die Alte Oper ist zertifizierter ‚ÖKOPROFIT Betrieb Frankfurt am Main' 2009/2010. Im Zuge dessen verfügt das Haus über energiesparende Büroausstattung und LED-Lampen, wasserlose Urinale sowie neuste Gebäudetechnik für Klimatisierung, Heizen und Kühlen.

Wir lassen den ‚vorbildlichen Bau im Lande Hessen 1982' links von uns und gehen geradeaus, die Große Bockenheimer Straße entlang. So heißt die gepflasterte Fußgängerzone zwischen Opernplatz und Börsenstraße offiziell, für die Frankfurter ist es schlicht die ‚Fressgass': Hier reiht sich ein Restaurant, ein Feinkostladen und ein Café an das andere – flankiert von noblen Boutiquen und Geschäften.

Wir folgen der Straße, nun **Kalbächer Gasse**, weiter. An der Börsenstraße biegen wir links ab, dann rechts und erreichen den 1874–79 errichteten Monumentalbau der Wertpapierbörse. Am anderen Ende des **Börsenplatzes** symbolisieren die Bronzestatuen Bulle und Bär (1987, Reinhard Dachlauer) steigende und fallende Kurse. An ihnen gehen wir links in die Schillerstraße und überqueren diese etwa in der Mitte des Börsengebäudes. Durch eine Gasse in der

in 'ÖKOPROFIT' a project run by the city of Frankfurt for small and medium enterprises to practise environmental management. The goal is to consume less energy and fewer recources as a result of the development and implementation of practical in-house specific measures. This leads to lower operating costs and protects the environment by a total of more than 21,000 tons of CO_2 annually. The Alte Oper was awarded the certificate 'ÖKOPROFIT Betrieb Frankfurt am Main' for 2009/2010. This is due to initiatives such as energy-efficient office equipment and LED lighting, waterless urinals and newest technology for air conditioning, heating and cooling.

We leave the most 'ideal building in the State of Hesse 1982' to our left and walk along the Große Bockenheimer Straße. This is the official name of the cobbled pedestrian street between Opernplatz and Börsenstraße, for the locals, it is simply the 'Fressgass': Here one classical restaurant, deli or coffee shop is lined up next to another and flanked by posh boutiques and shops.

We follow the **Kalbächer Gasse** further. On the Börsenstraße we turn left then right and arrive at the monumental Stock Exchange from 1874–79. At the other end of the **Börsenplatz**,

> Alte Oper:
>
> Characteristic, tip
> Guided tours for groups of 12 or more are available at the Alte Oper. The price is € 7 per person or fixed rate € 84 with smaller groups.
> Contact:
> Michael Dückers
> Phone: 01578 5521-843
> 9.00 am – 3.00 pm
> E-Mail: fuehrungen@alteoper.de
> www.alteoper.de

> Popular is the Fressgass Festival in June and the Rheingau Wine Festival in August.

Palais Quartier/Palais district

Eschenheimer Turm/Tower

Schneller Zugang zum Aussichtspunkt: Links neben der ‚Zeilgalerie' gelangen wir über den Eingang zum Cinemagnum direkt 3D-Kino direkt zum Aufzug, der zur Panorama-Plattform Skydeck führt. Von ihr eröffnet sich ein faszinierender Blick auf Frankfurt.

Nach einem Architekturwettbewerb in 2002 wurde die Peterskirche von 2004–2007 im Inneren umgestaltet. Der Hauptsaal des Kirchenschiffs bietet Platz für unterschiedlichste Veranstaltungen mit bis zu 1.000 Personen. Die Kirche wurde 2008 als ein vorbildlicher Bau im Land Hessen prämiert.

Blockrandbebauung kommen wir auf die **Große Eschenheimer Straße**, direkt auf das **Palais Thurn und Taxis** zu. Es wurde 1739 von Robert de Cotte, dem Hofarchitekten des Sonnenkönigs Ludwig XIV., fertig gestellt. Das im 2. Weltkrieg stark beschädigte Gebäude wurde bei der Neugestaltung des Areals in 2010 verkleinert wiederaufgebaut. Dahinter steht der 135 m hohe **Nextower** (*DGNB*-Zertifikat in Gold 2011). Mit seiner geknickten Glas-Aluminium-Fassade ist er das Wahrzeichen des neuen **Palais Quartiers**. Es besteht aus dem Büroturm, dem Shoppingcenter My Zeil, dem Hotel Jumeirah Frankfurt und dem Palais selbst. Links sehen wir den **Eschenheimer Turm**, ein Stadttor aus dem 15. Jahrhundert. Wir lassen das älteste weitgehend original erhaltene Bauwerk der Frankfurter Innenstadt hinter uns und wenden uns der **Hauptwache** zu. Das ursprünglich 1728 errichtete barocke Gebäude, einst Polizeistation und Gefängnis, gab dem angrenzenden Platz seinen Namen. Links sehen wir die 1954 wieder aufgebaute, evangelische **Katharinenkirche** mit Flankenturm und barocken Zierportalen, ein ursprünglich 1678–81 errichteter Saalbau. Wir begeben uns links in das Getümmel der **Zeil** mit ihren Kaufhäusern, Läden und Cafés. Die auf der ‚**Zeilgalerie**' öffentlich zugängliche Dachterrasse ermöglicht einen Blick auf die Skyline und die Kirchen der Stadt. Ein paar Schritte später sehen wir links die trichterförmig eingewölbte Glasfassade des 2009 eröffneten ‚**MyZeil**', die den Besucher förmlich in die Einkaufspassage mit einer 46 m langen, freitragenden Rolltreppe hineinzuziehen scheint. Wir lassen uns auf der Zeil weiter nach Osten treiben. Am 1984 von Lutz Brockhaus erstellten ‚Frankfurter-Figuren-Brunnen' aus weißem Carraramarmor halten wir uns links und folgen der Brönner- bis zur Stephanstraße. Schräg rechts entdecken wir auf einem Plateau die **Jugend-**

the bronze statues of the Bull and Bear (1987, Reinhard Dachlauer) symbolize rising and falling prices. At the statues we turn left in the Schillerstraße and cross it at about the middle of the stock exchange building. Through an alley in the block development we come to the **Große Eschenheimer Straße** directly opposite the **Palais Thurn und Taxis**. It was completed in 1739 by Robert de Cotte, the court architect of the Sonnenkönig (Sun King) Louis XIV. The building which was badly damaged and rebuilt on a reduced area in the redesign of the site in 2010. Behind it is the 135m high **Nextower** (*DGNB* Certificate in Gold 2011). With his curved glass and aluminium facade, it is the symbol of the new **Palais district**. It consists of the office tower, the shopping centre, My Zeil, the Jumeirah Frankfurt hotel and the Palais itself. On the left we see the **Eschenheimer Tower**, a city gate from the 15th Century. We leave Frankfurt's oldest surviving building in its original state behind us and turn our attention to the **Hauptwache**. The baroque building originally built in 1728, which gave its name to the adjacent square, was formerly the police station and jail. On the left is the Protestant **Catherine's Church**, originally erected in the years 1678–81 as a large hall and which in 1954 was rebuilt with flanking tower and baroque ornamental portals. We go left into the bustle of the Zeil with its department stores, shops and cafes. The roof terrace of the publicly accessible **'Zeilgalerie'** offers a view of the skyline and the city's churches.

A few steps further on, we see on the left, the funnel vaulted glass facade of **'MyZeil'** which opened in 2009. Visitors seem literally drawn into the shopping centre with a 46m long, cantilevered escalator. We allow ourselves to saunter along the Zeil in an easterly direction. At

> Quick access to the lookout point: To the left of the 'Zeilgalerie' from the Cinemagnum 3D cinema entrance hall we have direct access to the elevator that leads to the panoramic platform Sky deck from which a fascinating view of Frankfurt can be seen.

> After an architectural competition in 2002, the interior of the Peterskirche was remodelled from 2004–2007. The nave can accommodate a variety of events of up to 1,000 people. In 2008 the church was awarded a prize as an exemplary building in the State of Hesse.

Stiftung Waisenhaus

Kultur-Kirche St. Peter in einem ruhigen Park, dem alten **Petersfriedhof**. Diesen betreten wir durch ein Gittertor. Seine Grabmäler von 1452 bis 1828 spiegeln Geschichten über Frankfurt und seine bekannten Familien, wie die Nestlés, Goethes oder Bethmanns, wieder. Wir laufen zur Peterskirche hinauf. Im späten 19. Jahrhundert errichtet und 1965 wieder aufgebaut, bietet sie heute einen attraktiven Veranstaltungsort, der eine Brücke zwischen Kirche, Jugendlichen und Kulturen baut.

Wir verlassen das Plateau und gehen die **Bleichstraße** nach rechts. Bei Nr. 10, dem Verwaltungs- und Betreuungszentrum der **Stiftung Waisenhaus**, stoppen wir. Ihr neues Domizil mit hocheffizienter Pelletheizungsanlage und Absorptionskältemaschine ist das erste zertifizierte Büro-*Passivhaus* Frankfurts. Es wurde 2009 mit dem Preis ‚Energieoptimiertes Bauen – Architektur mit Energie' des Bundesministeriums für Wirtschaft und Technologie ausgezeichnet. In das Untergeschoss wurden gut erhaltene Reste der städtischen Verteidigungsanlage mit einer Sternschanze aus dem 16. Jahrhundert integriert. Die Zweiteilung der gemauerten Natursteinfassade zeigt die historische Parzellierung. Wir folgen der Bleichstraße bis zur nächsten Kreuzung. Dort halten wir uns links, um an der

---

Scheffelhof:
Teamarbeit für umfassende Nachhaltigkeit

Scheffelhof:

Bauherr / Client
Baugruppe Scheffelhof GbR, private Bauherrengemeinschaft aus 10 Familien/
Private building owners' association consisting of 10 families

Architekt / Architect
ROOK architekten, Frankfurt am Main

Baujahr /
Year of construction
2007–2008

Nutzfläche/Useful area
1.462 m²

Westend – City Centre | 4

the 'Frankfurter-Figuren-Brunnen' created by Lutz Brockhaus in 1984 in white Carrera marble, we bear left and follow the Brönnerstraße to the Stephanstraße. Diagonally and to the right in a quiet park, the old **St. Peter's Cemetery**, we discover on a plateau, the **Jugend-Kultur-Kirche St. Peter** (youth culture Church of St. Peter). This we enter through a gate. Its tombs from 1452 to 1828 reflect stories of Frankfurt and its well-known families, such as Nestlé, Goethe or Bethmann. We walk up to St. Peter's Church. Originally built in the late 19th Century and rebuilt in 1965, today it offers an attractive venue and acts as a bridge between the church, youth and different cultures.

We leave the plateau and go right on **Bleichstraße.** We stop at number 10, the administration and supervision of the **Stiftung Waisenhaus** (Orphanage Foundation Centre). Its new domicile, with a highly efficient pellet heating system and an absorption cooler, is the first certified *Passive House* office building in Frankfurt. It was awarded the 'Energy-Optimized Construction – Architecture with Energy' by the Federal Ministry of Economics and Technology in 2009. Well-preserved ruins of the city defence system like the Sternschanze from the 16th Century have been integrated into

Stiftung Waisenhaus

Scheffelhof:
Team work for all encompassing durabilty

Scheffelhof:
Energetic Level
| *Passive Houses*
| Awarded as *'Green Building Frankfurt'* in 2009

Use (renewable) energy
| Solar system for hot water (storage)
| Compact ventilation system with a *heat recovery* rate of over 85% for the heating and ventilation
| Natural lighting and ventilation
| Partial purchase of green electricity

Characteristic, tip
Due to the large windows and despite the central location optimal light conditions prevail in all areas. This ensures comfort and solar benefits during colder periods.
The district is part of the pilot project 'Vernetzte Spiel- und Begegnungsräume' (Networked game and meeting rooms) of Frankfurt's transport department in cooperation with the Federal Office for Building and Planning

Westend – Innenstadt

Scheffelhof:

Energetisches Niveau
| *Passivhäuser*
| Auszeichnung als ‚Green Building Frankfurt' in 2009

Nutzung (erneuerbarer) Energien
| Solaranlage für Warmwasser(speicher)
| Kompaktlüftungsanlage mit einem *Wärmerückgewinnungs*grad von über 85% für die Beheizung und Lüftung
| Natürliche Belichtung und Belüftung
| Teilweise Bezug von Ökostrom

Besonderheit, Tipp
Über die großen Fensterflächen sind trotz Innenstadtlage in allen Räumen optimale Belichtungsverhältnisse gegeben. Dies sorgt für Wohnkomfort und solare Gewinne in der Heizperiode. Das Quartier ist Teil des Modellprojektes ‚Vernetzte Spiel- und Begegnungsräume' des Frankfurter Verkehrsdezernates in Kooperation mit dem Bundesamt für Bauwesen und Raumordnung.

Zoo Frankfurt:

Bernhard-Grzimek-Allee 1

Geöffnet/Open
9.00–19.00 Uhr (Sommer)
9.00–17.00 Uhr (Winter)

Ecke Friedberger Tor/Eschenheimer Anlage links den Grünzug entlang zu schlendern. An seiner Links-Kurve orientieren wir uns rechts in die Scheffelstraße und sehen links an der Mercatorstraße die katholische Kirche St. Bernhard, erbaut 1905–07 sowie in der Nachkriegszeit und 1994 renoviert. Wir laufen einen schmalen Weg auf sie zu und erreichen den **Scheffelhof**.

Hier, im beliebten Stadtteil Nordend, entstanden auf engem Raum 10 familiengerechte, nachhaltige Reihen- und Doppelhäuser aus Kalksandstein. Mit hoher gestalterischer und funktionaler Qualität erfüllt der **Scheffelhof** auch die Ansprüche der Stadtentwicklung nach Verdichtung und Aufwertung der Innenstadt. Die 2,5-geschossigen Gebäude mit von 125 bis 175 m^2 großen Wohneinheiten befinden sich im Blockinneren zwischen **Koselstraße, Scheffelstraße** und **Friedberger Landstraße**. Sie orientieren sich zu einem privaten Hof und stehen aus Belichtungsgründen versetzt zueinander. Die Dachgärten und -terrassen sowie die Hofbegrünung verbessern das städtische Kleinklima.

Wir gehen zur Mercatorstraße zurück und folgen ihr bis zu ihrem Ende. So wieder am Friedberger Tor angelangt, überqueren wir die Friedberger Landstraße sowie die Friedberger Anlage und biegen dann links in den Grünzug ein. Hier nehmen wir den mittleren Parkweg – an Schiller Eiche, Bethmannweiher und Rinz-Denkmal rechts vorbei – bis er auf die Zeil trifft. Wenn wir uns hier links halten würden, kämen wir über die Pfingstweidstraße direkt auf den Alfred-Brehm-Platz im Ostend zu. Dort befindet sich der **Frankfurter Zoo** mit dem Fritz Rémond Theater. Der 1858 gegründete zoologische Garten gehört zu den ältesten der Welt. Zu sehen sind Löwen, Nashörner, Giraffen, Krokodile, Affen – kurz die beeindruckende Tierwelt Afrikas und

Scheffelhof

the basement. The historical fragmentation can be seen on the two sections of the brick stone facade.

We follow the Bleichstraße to the next junction. At the corner Friedberger Tor/Eschenheimer Anlage we stroll along the left side of the grassed area. In the left-hand curve we turn right into Scheffelstraße and see to the left in the Mercatorstraße the Catholic Church of St. Bernard, built in 1905–07 and renovated after WW II and in 1994. We walk the narrow path towards it and arrive at the **Scheffelhof.**

Here, in the popular district of Nordend, 10 family-friendly, sustainable terraced and semi-detached houses of sand-lime brick were built in the confined space. With top design and functional quality the **Scheffelhof** meets the urban development demands of concentration and enhancement of the city centre. The 2.5-storey building, with residential units ranging in size from 125m^2 to 175m^2, are located within the block between **Koselstraße, Scheffelstraße** and **Friedberger Landstraße**. They are arranged around a private courtyard and are offset from each other in order to optimize light conditions. The roof gardens and terraces as well as the courtyard vegetation improve the urban microclimate.

Ludwig-Börne-Schule/School

Am Donnerstag und Samstag lohnt es sich, den Bauernmarkt an der Konstablerwache zu besuchen. Von frischem Obst über eine gute Flasche Wein bis hin zu regionalen Spezialitäten wie die Frankfurter Grüne Soße ist alles dabei – direkt vom Erzeuger.

anderer Kontinente. Im Freigelände und in einzigartigen Tierhäusern werden 500 verschiedene Arten und über 4.500 Tiere präsentiert.

Wir laufen an der Zeil rechts und dann an der nächsten Kreuzung links. Nach wenigen Metern erreichen wir die **Ludwig-Börne-Schule**. Der städtische Gebäudekomplex in der **Lange Straße 30–36** nimmt die vorhandenen Fluchten auf und vermeidet jährlich 8,5 t CO_2: Er wurde 2011 auf *Passivhaus*standard saniert und erweitert und bekam dabei ein einheitliches Erscheinungsbild. Variierende, gekippte Fensterleibungen bilden eine plastische Fassade, die den Sonneneinfall in die Klassenräume lenkt. Die farbliche Konzeption der Innenräume stammt aus dem Atelier des Schweizer Farbkünstlers Jörg Niederberger. Wir begeben uns zurück zur Zeil und halten uns links. An Gerichtsgebäuden vorbei gelangen wir so zum Platz Konstablerwache.

We go back to Mercatorstraße and follow it to its end. We are now back at the Friedberger Tor, we cross Friedberger Landstrasse and Friedberger Anlage and then turn left into the grassy area. Here we take the middle path – go past the Schiller Eiche, the Bethmann pond and the Rinz monument on the left – until we reach the **Zeil**. If we kept left here, via Pfingstweidstraße, we would arrive directly at the Alfred-Brehm-Platz in the Ostend. There the **Frankfurt Zoo** with the Fritz Rémond Theatre is located. Founded in 1858, the zoo is one of the oldest in the world. There are lions, rhinos, giraffes, crocodiles, monkeys – in short, a very impressive wildlife from Africa and other continents. In outdoor enclosures and in unique animal houses, the zoo presents a total of 500 different species and more than 4,500 animals.

We go right on the Zeil and then left at the next crossing. After a few meters we reach the **Ludwig-Börne-School**. The urban complex in the **Lange Straße 30–36** annually avoids 8.5 tons of CO_2. In 2011, it was renovated and extended to *passive house* standard and since then has a uniform appearance. Varying tilted window jambs form a three-dimensional facade that directs the sunlight into the classrooms. The interior colour design is from the studio of the Swiss artist Jörg Niederberger. We go back to the Zeil and keep to the left. We pass by the court buildings and thus reach the Konstablerwache.

On Thursdays and Saturdays it is well worth visiting the farmers' market at Konstablerwache. Here you can find everything from fresh fruit to a nice bottle of wine or regional specialties like the Frankfurter Grüne Soße (green herbal sauce) – all directly from the producer.

5 | City

Route City – Innenstadt und Altstadt

Die vollständig bebauten Gebiete Innenstadt und Altstadt erstrecken sich am rechten Mainufer, innerhalb der begrünten Frankfurter Wallanlagen, die durch die 1827 erlassene Wallservitut (Satzung zum Schutz öffentlicher Grünanlagen) vor Bebauung geschützt werden. Das Stadtbild ist heute maßgeblich durch den Wiederaufbau nach dem zweiten Weltkrieg geprägt, was die Rekonstruktion zahlreicher prominenter Gebäude und Plätze einschließt.

Unsere Route beginnt an der Hauptwache. Eine trichterförmige Treppenanlage führt zum unterirdischen ÖPNV-Anschluss samt Einkaufspassage. Dort sehen wir auf Höhe der Schillerstraße die Bronzefiguren des von Franziska Lenz-Gerhard geschaffenen Struwwelpeter-Brunnens, der hier seit 1985 an den Arzt und Dichter Heinrich Hoffmann erinnert. Wir folgen der Biebergasse bis zum Rathenauplatz und entdecken am südlichen Rand den Anfang der Goethestraße, einer eleganten Einkaufsstraße.

Der Platz geht fließend in den mit Bäumen bepflanzten Goetheplatz über. An seinem Beginn erkennen wir ein Standbild für den berühmten Dichter (1844, Ludwig von Schwanthaler). Der Platz erweitert sich nach Süden zum Roßmarkt mit dem Johannes-Gutenberg-Denkmal (1858, Eduard Schmidt von der Launitz).

Wir biegen rechts in die Junghofstraße ein und erreichen bei Nr. 18–26 unser erstes Ziel. Der **Junghof** im östlichen Banken- und Business-Viertel bietet mit seinem Mix aus moderner Architektur und historischen Stilelementen ein besonderes Ambiente. So zeigt er sich in den neuen verglasten Obergeschossen mit einem Aluminium-Bogendach extravagant, im Eckgebäude Neue Mainzer Straße hingegen traditionsbetont. Der denkmalgeschützte Bau

---

Innenstadt:

Der 1333 gegründete Bezirk, auch Neustadt genannt, ist das Handels- und Geschäftszentrum von Frankfurt. Es wird im Süden durch den Main begrenzt und umgibt die heutige Altstadt.

Auf der unteren Ebene der Hauptwache gibt es sowohl einen zentralen Fahrkartenverkauf als auch den Shop ‚Frankfurt Ticket RheinMain', der Eintrittskarten für verschiedenste Events in und um Frankfurt anbietet.

Von der Goethestraße lässt sich die Kleine Bockenheimer Straße erschließen. In der Nummer 18a befindet sich der 1952 eröffnete Jazzkeller.

Der ‚JUNGHOF':

Zusammenspiel von Alt und Neu plus LEED-Zertifizierung in Gold

Tour City – City Centre and Historic District

The built-up areas of the city centre and the old town extend along the right bank of the River Main within the green Frankfurt ramparts which are protected from development due to 'Wallservitut', a decree from 1827 (statute for the protection of public parks). Today, the city is heavily influenced by the redevelopment after the Second World War including the reconstruction of many prominent buildings and squares.

Our route starts at the Hauptwache. A funnel-shaped staircase leads to the underground and a shopping arcade.
At Schillerstraße the Struwwelpeter Fountain with its bronze figures, created by Franziska Lenz-Gerhard in 1985, is a memorial to the physician and poet Heinrich Hoffmann. We follow the Biebergasse to the Rathenauplatz and discover on its southern edge the start of the Goethestraße, an elegant shopping street.
The square opens up into the tree-lined Goetheplatz where we see a statue of Goethe, the famous poet, created by Ludwig von

City Centre:

The district, also called New Town, was founded in 1333; it is the commercial and business centre of Frankfurt bordered to the south by the River Main and surrounds the present old town.

On the lower level of the Station, Hauptwache, tickets for local transport can be bought. There is also the shop ‚Frankfurt Ticket Rhein-Main', which sells tickets for various events in and around Frankfurt.

From Goethestraße, you can turn into Kleine Bockenheimer Straße. At number 18a is the 'Jazz-keller' which opened in 1952.

5 | City

Junghof:

Bauherr / Client
Helaba Landesbank
Hessen-Thüringen

Architekt / Architect
schneider+schumacher,
Frankfurt am Main

**Baujahr /
Year of construction**
2000–2003

Nutzfläche/Useful area
23.500 m²

Junghof:

Energetisches Niveau
| LEED-Zertifizierung
  in Gold 2012 für
  Bestandsgebäude:
  Betrieb und Instand-
  haltung

**Nutzung (erneuer-
barer) Energien**
| Versorgung mit
  Ökostrom
| Natürliche Belichtung
  und Belüftung
| Einsatz intelligenter
  Gebäudetechnik

Besonderheit, Tipp
| Belluga Saloon für
  Mittagspause und
  Nachtleben
| Power Plate Studio
  für Fitness und
  Gesundheit
| Grüner Hof als kleine,
  grüne Erholungszone

Junghof

wurde um 1873 als Zentralstelle der Deutschen Reichsbank errichtet. Die optische und logistische Trennung des Karrees in einzelne Baukörper setzt sich auch in der Innenarchitektur fort: Von der herrschaftlichen Gründerzeit, über die klassische 50er-Jahre-Moderne bis hin zum Stil des 21. Jahrhunderts. Gemeinsam sind ihnen großzügige lichte Raumhöhen von mindestens 2,75 m und eine moderne Gebäudetechnik, wie Kühldecken bis in das 5. Obergeschoss. Gleichzeitig weist der außen mit Naturstein verkleidete Junghof eine gute Energiebilanz auf und ist – nach dem Main Tower – die 2. Bestandsimmobilie in Deutschland, die über ein LEED-Zertifikat in Gold verfügt. Hierbei wurden neben den gebäudetechnischen Eigenschaften auch zahlreiche Nachhaltigkeitskriterien für eine umweltfreundliche und ressourcenschonende Nutzung nachgewiesen. So dient die Gebäudeleittechnik als Erfassungs-, Monitoring- und Optimierungssystem. Das Lichtspiel in den Fenstern mit Wärme- und teilweise mit Sonnenschutz-Isolierglas gibt den Innenhöfen einen eigenen Charakter. Wir folgen dem Straßenverlauf bis zum Eurotheum und biegen links in die Neue Mainzer Straße ein. Durch Arkaden gelangen wir bei Nr. 52–58 zu unserem nächsten Ziel. Das durch Baubronze betonte Raster des quadratischen Vertikalbaus

Junghof

Schwanthaler in 1844. The plaza expands in a southerly direction towards the Roßmarkt with the Johannes Gutenberg monument created by Edward Schmidt of Launitz in 1858.

We turn right into Junghofstraße and reach at No. 18–26 our first goal. The **Junghof** creates a unique atmosphere in the eastern banking and business district with its mix of modern architecture and period features. The building is unusual in its appearance with its aluminium domed roof over the new glazed upper floors but the corner building on Neue Mainzer Straße is traditional. The heritage-listed building was constructed around 1873 as the headquarters of the German Reichsbank. The optical and logistic separation of the square into individual parts is also reflected in the interior design, from the stately early days to the classical 50's through to the modern style of the 21st Century. They all have in common a generous ceiling height of at least 2.75m and modern building technology in common such as ceiling cooling systems up to the 5th floor.

The Junghof with its exterior cladding of natural stone is very energy-efficient and is – after the Main Tower – the 2nd existing property in Germany, which has a *LEED* Gold Certificate. In addition to the building's technical

The 'JUNGHOF':

Interaction of old and new, plus LEED Certificate in Gold

Junghof:

Energetic level
| *LEED* Certificate in Gold for existing buildings in 2012: Operation and Maintenance

Use (renewable) energy
| Supply of green electricity
| Natural ventilation and light
| Use of intelligent building technology

Characteristic, tip
| Belluga Saloon for lunch and Nightlife
| Power Plate Studio for Fitness and Health
| Green Yard as a small, green recreation zone

Der ‚MAIN TOWER':
Deutschlands erstes Bestandgebäude mit LEED-Zertifizierung in Gold

Main Tower:

Bauherr / Client
Helaba Landesbank
Hessen-Thüringen

Architekt / Architect
ASP Schweger & Partner
Architekten, Hamburg

Baujahr /
Year of construction
1996–1999

Nutzfläche/Useful area
62.000 m²

Main Tower:

Energetisches Niveau
| *LEED*-Zertifizierung
  in Gold 2011 für
  Bestandsgebäude:
  Betrieb und Instandhaltung

Nutzung (erneuerbarer) Energien
| Versorgung mit
  Ökostrom
| Möglichkeit der
  Energieversorgung
  durch *Blockheizkraftwerk* und Erdwärmesystem
| Natürliche Belichtung
  und Belüftung
| Einsatz intelligenter
  Gebäudetechnik

bildet ein klares gestalterisches Gegengewicht zum runden Teil des **Main Tower**. Im Sockelbereich wurde als weiterer Kontrast die denkmalgeschützte Fassade des Vorgängerbaus integriert. Im Foyer sind zwei Kunstwerke für die Öffentlichkeit zugänglich: Die Videoinstallation ‚The World of Appearances' (2000, Bill Viola) und das Wandmosaik ‚Frankfurter Treppe/XX. Jahrhundert' (1999, Stephan Huber). Durch die Lastabtragung über eine Kernstruktur aus Stahlbeton und außen liegende Stahlstützen wurde mit dem etwa 200 m hohen Rundturm erstmals in Europa ein Hochhaus mit komplett verglaster Fassade realisiert. Dabei konnte auf eine Vollklimatisierung verzichtet werden: Die 2.550 Fenster zur Licht- und Luftversorgung der Büros lassen sich parallel zur Fassade nach außen öffnen und sind mit der jeweiligen Technik gekoppelt.

Main Tower

Main Tower

characteristics numerous sustainability criteria for an environmentally and resource friendly usage were proven. The building control system serves as a sensing, monitoring and optimization system. The play of light in the windows, some with heat insulation glazing and some with solar protection glazing, gives the courtyards a special character.

We follow the road to the Eurotheum and turn left into the Neue Mainzer Straße. Through the arcades we reach our next destination, No. 52–58. The architectural bronze cladding emphasises the square shaped building, a creative contrast to the round part of the **Main Tower**. As a second contrast the listed facade of the former building has been integrated in the dado. In the foyer, there are two artworks displayed for the public: the video installation, 'The World of Appearances' (2000, Bill Viola) and the wall mosaic, 'Frankfurter Treppe/XX. Jahrhundert' (1999, Stephan Huber). Due to the load transfer via a core structure made of reinforced concrete and exterior steel columns a 200m high roundel could be constructed, for the first time in Europe, as a high-rise with a fully glazed facade.

Thus, it was possible to dispense with full climate control: The 2,550 windows which

The ‚MAIN TOWER':
First existing building in Germany with LEED-Gold-Certification

Main Tower:
Energetic level
| *LEED* Certificate in Gold for existing buildings in 2011: Operation and Maintenance

Use (renewable) energy
| Supply of green electricity
| Possibility of energy supply through *cogeneration* and geothermal system
| Natural ventilation and light
| Use of intelligent building technology

Characteristic, tip
The top of the tower has a visitor platform at a height of 200m. It is the highest public vantage point in Frankfurt and offers a panoramic view over the city and the region. Access to it is via the Neue Mainzer Straße. Also located on the 53rd Floor is the Main Tower Restaurant & Bar with lounge and a TV studio of 'Hessischer Rundfunk' (Hessen Radio).

5 | City

Main Tower:

Besonderheit, Tipp
Die Spitze des Turms bildet eine Besucherterrasse in rund 200 m Höhe. Sie ist der höchste öffentlich zugängliche Aussichtspunkt in Frankfurt und bietet einen Rundumblick über die Stadt und die Region. Der Zugang dazu ist die Neue Mainzer Straße. Außerdem befinden sich im 53. Geschoss das Main Tower Restaurant & Bar mit Lounge und Café sowie ein TV-Studio des Hessischen Rundfunks.

Commerzbank-Hochhaus:

Das erste ‚Green Building' der Welt

Commerzbank-Hochhaus:

Bauherr / Client
Commerzbank AG

Architekt / Architect
Lord Norman Foster
Büro ‚Foster and Partners', London

**Baujahr /
Year of construction**
1994–1997

Nutzfläche/Useful area
52.700 m²

Somit setzte das Gebäude bereits bei seiner Fertigstellung 1999 architektonische und energetische Standards. 2011 erhielt der Main Tower als erstes Bestandsgebäude in Deutschland ein *LEED*-Zertifikat in Gold für Betrieb und Instandhaltung: Das Hochhaus mit 56 Obergeschossen besitzt eine moderne Gebäudetechnik, verfügt über eine intelligente Energieversorgung und geht schonend mit natürlichen Ressourcen um. So dienen rund 50 der insgesamt 112 Gründungspfähle als Erdwärmesystem, das den Boden als Energiespeicher nutzt.

Rechts vor uns sehen wir in der imposanten Hochhausschlucht das Japan Center mit seiner Fassade aus gestrahltem roten Granit und seinem auskragenden Dach. Wir laufen an der Baustelle des Taunus Turms vorbei, links in die Kaiserstraße und erreichen so ein weiteres Ziel. In der Innenstadt prägt der Stahlskelettbau der **Commerzbank-Zentrale** die Skyline. Vom Kaiserplatz aus betritt der Besucher den rund 259 m hohen Turm über einen verglasten Treppenaufgang. Im 1. Geschoss lädt eine großzügig gestaltete Plaza mit Restaurant zum Verweilen ein. Über der sich anschließenden Lobby steigt das 160 m hohe Atrium empor. Um dieses gruppieren sich 45 Büro-Etagen. Die Versorgungskerne befinden sich in den Ecken des Grundrisses: Ein abgerundetes, gleichschenkliges Dreieck mit leicht nach außen gewölbten Seiten. Der Entwurf aus den frühen 1990er Jahren nahm – mit seinen bis in die obersten Geschosse zu öffnenden Fenstern und seiner technischen Ausstattung, die unter anderem das Tageslicht stark berücksichtigt – den Begriff des ‚Green Building' vorweg. „Der Commerzbank-Turm in Frankfurt am Main", so Lord Norman Foster in einer Publikation des Bundesumweltministeriums, „ist ein symbolhaft und funktional ‚grünes' Gebäude. Obwohl es über eine Klimasteuerung

Commerzbank-Zentrale

provide the offices with light and air can be opened outwards, parallel to the facade and are constructed with the appropriate technique. The building set architectural and energetical standards at its completion in 1999. In 2011, the Main Tower was the first existing building in Germany which received a *LEED* Gold certificate for operation and maintenance: The high-rise with 56-storeys incorporates modern building technology, an intelligent power supply and preserves natural resources. For example, approximately 50 of the in total 112 original piles are part of the geothermal system which uses the ground as energy storage.

Between the impressive high-rises we see on the right the Japan Centre with its burnished red granite facade and its cantilevered roof. We walk past the construction area of the Taunus Tower and turn left into the Kaiserstraße, where we reach our next goal.

The city centre's skyline is dominated by the steel frame construction of the **Commerzbank-Zentrale**. From the Kaiserplatz the visitor enters, via a glass staircase, the approximately 259m high tower. On the 1st floor a spacious plaza with restaurant invites you to take a break. A 160m high atrium rises up over the adjacent lobby around which 45 office floors are arranged.

Commerzbank-Tower:
The world's first 'Green Building'

Commerzbank-Tower:
Energetic level
| Awarded as *'Green Building Frankfurt'* in 2009

Use (renewable) energy
| Use of innovative and environment-friendly building technology
| Natural ventilation and the tower gardens place particular emphasis on additional eco-logical aspects
| Since 2008: purchase of green electricity

5 | City

Commerzbank-Hochhaus:

Energetisches Niveau
| Auszeichnung der Stadt Frankfurt als ‚Green Building Frankfurt' 2009

Nutzung (erneuerbarer) Energien
| Einsatz innovativer und umweltfreundlicher Gebäudetechnik
| Zusätzliche ökologische Akzente setzen die natürliche Be- und Entlüftung sowie die Turmgärten
| Seit Anfang 2008: Bezug von Ökostrom

Besonderheit, Tipp
Besuchergruppen genießen regelmäßig den großartigen Blick über die Stadt, den Deutschlands höchstes Bürogebäude ihnen bietet. Führungen sind kostenfrei und finden an jedem letzten Samstag im Monat stündlich von 10.00–17.00 Uhr statt. Eine Voranmeldung ist notwendig. Aufgrund des großen Interesses besteht bei der Terminvergabe eine relativ lange Vorlaufzeit. Informationen zur Anmeldung finden Sie unter: www.tinyurl.com/a4yu96f

verfügt, nutzt es ein natürliches Lüftungssystem zur Reduktion des Energieverbrauchs, was es zum weltweit ersten ökologischen Hochhaus macht." Wichtig für die Frischluftversorgung sind neun Gärten. Sie schrauben sich spiralförmig in die Höhe. Jeweils drei sind nach einer Himmelsrichtung orientiert und thematisch geordnet: Asiatische Vegetation im Osten, mediterrane im Süden und nordamerikanische im Westen. Jede Etage verfügt über drei Flügel. Zwei sind Bürofläche, der dritte gehört zu einem der viergeschossigen Gärten. Sie dienen gleichzeitig als Kommunikationszonen für die Mitarbeiter und lassen Tageslicht in die innen liegenden Räume. Diese raffinierte Gestaltung gibt dem Turm eine große Offenheit. Seine elegante Erscheinung wird noch durch eine weltweit einmalige Rahmenkonstruktion verstärkt: Sie überspannt die über 34 m breiten Gärten stützenfrei. Eindrucksvoll ist auch die Gründung: Der Bau steht auf 111 Stahlbetonpfählen. Sie haben einen Mindestdurchmesser von 1,5 m und ragen bis zu 48,5 m tief in den Boden. Die Fassade setzt sich aus zwei Schalen zusammen, zwischen denen die Luft frei zirkuliert. Die Büros lassen sich zu mehr als 3/4 des Jahres natürlich belüften. Nur bei extremen Witterungen übernimmt die Gebäude-Leittechnik mit einer Lüftungsanlage die Versorgung. Die Nutzer können ihr Raumklima weitgehend individuell steuern. Geheizt wird mit konventionellen Heizkörpern. Die integrierten Kühldecken werden umweltfreundlich aus *Kraft-Wärme-Kopplung* gespeist. Das für die Kühlung eingesetzte Frischwasser steht später für die Toilettenspülung zur Verfügung. Nicht nur Menschen schätzen den Turm: Seit 2007 brüten regelmäßig Wanderfalken ganz oben auf der Commerzbank-Zentrale.

Neben dem Kaiser-Brunnen von 1876 mit seinem großen Becken und kelchartigem Pfeiler

Maintenance shafts are located in the corners of the floor plan: A rounded, isosceles triangle with slightly outwardly curved sides. The design of the early 1990s was a forerunner for 'green buildings' with the facilty to open the windows all the way up to the top and its technical equipment which amongst other things takes the daylight factors strongly into account. "The Commerzbank Tower in Frankfurt is a symbolic and functional green building." according to Sir Norman Foster in a publication by the Federal Environmental Ministry, "Although it has a climate control system, it uses a natural ventilation system for the reduction of energy consumption, making it the world's first ecological high-rise." The nine gardens which spiral upwards are important for the fresh air supply. In groups of three, the gardens are oriented in a specific direction and thematically classified: Asian vegetation in the East, Mediterranean in the South and North American in the West. Each floor has three wings of which two are for office space and the third is one of the four-storey gardens. These also serve as communication areas for the employees and allow daylight into the interior. This clever design gives the tower a feeling of spaciousness. Its elegant appearance is further enhanced by a frame design which is unique: It spans the 34m wide gardens without pillars. The foundation is also impressive: The building stands on 111 reinforced concrete piles which have a minimum diameter of 1.5m and are up to 48.5m deep in the ground. The facade consists of two shells between which air can circulate freely. The offices can be naturally ventilated for more than 3/4 of the year. Only during extreme weather conditions does the building management control the supply with a ventilation system. The majority of the indoor climate can be controlled individually by the users. Heating is provided by

Commerzbank-Tower: Characteristic, tip

Groups of visitors regularly enjoy the grand view of the city, which Germany's highest office building offers them. Guided tours are free of charge and take place every hour on the last Saturday of the month from 10.00 am – 5.00 pm. Prior booking is required. Due to great interest in the tour, there is a relatively long waiting time. Registration information can be found at:
www.tinyurl.com/a4yu96f

5 | City

Helvetia Bürogebäude

Helvetia Bürogebäude:
Frühzeitig ganzheitliches und innovatives Gebäudekonzept

Helvetia Bürogebäude:

Bauherr / Client
Helvetia Schweizerische Versicherungsgesellschaft AG, Direktion für Deutschland

Architekt / Architect
Neumann Architekten GmbH, Frankfurt a. M.

Baujahr/Year of constr.
1998–2000

Nutzfläche/Useful area
4.100 m²

Energetisches Niveau
| Auszeichnung als ‚Green Building Frankfurt' in 2009

Nutzung (erneuerbarer) Energien
| Natürliche Lüftung und Belichtung
| Lüftungsanlage mit *Wärmerückgewinnung*

mit Schale sehen wir rechts das Junior-Haus (1951, Bauherr Kurt Junior). Die Eckfassade prägt ein rundes Glas-Treppenhaus. Wir gehen geradeaus auf die Dreiflügelanlage des Hotels Steigenberger Frankfurter Hof zu. Ursprünglich 1876 errichtet wurde es 1953 wieder aufgebaut. Wir überqueren die Kaiserstraße, folgen ihr nach links und biegen auf Höhe des Roßmarkts rechts in die Straße Am Salzhaus ab. Rechts, im Großen Hirschgraben, liegen das Volkstheater und das **Goethe-Haus** mit dem **Goethe-Museum**. Die originalgetreue Rekonstruktion des Geburtshauses des Dichters veranschaulicht die bürgerliche Wohnkultur des Spätbarocks. Wir gehen zurück und biegen nach rechts ab.
Auf einer schwierigen Grundstücksgeometrie entstand mit dem **Bürogebäude der Helvetia Versicherungen** in der Weißadlergasse 2 eine Architektur, bei der eine einfache und energieeffiziente Haustechnik exakt auf die bauphysikalisch hochwertige Konstruktion abgestimmt ist. Während der Bauphase wurde deren Ausführung extern überwacht und in den ersten zwei Jahren nach Bezug mit der Gebäudeleittechnik optimiert: Der Primärenergieverbrauch von rund 120 kWh/(m²a) ist noch heute vorbildlich. Die hochtransparente Fassade mit automatisierten Außenjalousien und Dreifachverglasungen sorgt für angenehm temperierte Innenräume, die mit Systemtrennwänden flexibel veränderbar sind. Bei der Materialwahl wurden langfristige ökologische Aspekte beachtet.
Wir folgen der Gasse bis zum Kornmarkt, halten uns rechts, gleich darauf an der Berliner Straße links, wo rechts der elliptische Zentralbau der **Paulskirche** in unser Blickfeld kommt. 1833 als evangelisch-lutherische Hauptkirche der Stadt erbaut, diente sie dann aber, mit ihrem damals größten und modernsten Saal Frankfurts, als Sitz für das 1. gesamtdeutsche Parlament. 1944

conventional radiators. The integrated ceiling cooling system is supplied by an environmentally friendly *combined heat and power* generation. The fresh water used for cooling is thereafter available for the toilet flushing system. The tower is not only appreciated by humans; since 2007 peregrine falcons regularly nest at the top of the Commerzbank headquarters.

Next to the Kaiserbrunnen from 1876 with its large basin and chalice-type pillars we see on the right the Junior-House (1951, owner Kurt Junior). The corner facade is characterised by a round glass staircase. We go straight towards the three winged Steigenberger Frankfurter Hof, which was originally built in 1876 and rebuilt in 1953. We cross the Kaiserstraße, follow it to the left and at Roßmarkt turn right into Am Salzhaus. On the right, in Großer Hirschgraben, are the National Theatre and the **Goethe House** with the **Goethe Museum**. The faithful reconstruction of the poet's birthplace provides an example of the bourgeois domestic culture of late Baroque. We retrace our steps and turn right.

The **Helvetia office building** was built on a strange shaped plot in the Weißadlergasse 2. This building has a simple and energy-efficient technology which is perfectly matched to the physical quality construction. External monitors overviewed its construction and this continued during the first two years of occupation. The primary energy consumption of about 120 kWh/(m²a) is still exemplary. The highly transparent facade with its automated external blinds and triple glazing ensures pleasantly tempered interiors that are flexibly changeable with system partitions. Long-term environmental issues were observed at the time when the material was chosen.

We follow the alley until we reach Kornmarkt, there wed keep to the right and directly

Helvetia office building

Helvetia office building:
Early holistic and innovative building concept

Helvetia office building:
Energetic level
| Awarded as *'Green Building Frankfurt'* in 2009

Use (renewable) energy
| Natural ventilation and lighting
| Ventilation system with a *heat recovery* system

Helvetia Bürogebäude: Besonderheit, Tipp
In dem Gebäude kam zum ersten Mal in Frankfurt eine thermoaktive *Bauteilaktivierung* (Betondecke) zur Anwendung. Mit ihr wird im Sommer ein angenehm kühles und im Winter ein warmes Raumklima geschaffen – zu 1/3 über den jeweiligen Boden und zu 2/3 über die Decke. Dafür wurde eine eigene Steuerung entwickelt, die die Trägheit des Systems und ihren Selbstregulierungseffekt berücksichtigt.

Heute ist die **Paulskirche** vor allem ein Ort der Erinnerung für den Beginn der deutschen Demokratie. Im Versammlungssaal im Obergeschoss werden beispielsweise der Internationale Hochhauspreis sowie der Goethepreis der Stadt Frankfurt verliehen.

Die Ost-West-Linie, die sogenannte Altstadtstrecke, der Straßenbahn ist bis heute in Betrieb. Dort fährt auch die Touristenattraktion ‚Ebbelwei-Expreß'.

wurde der Sandsteinbau zerstört und am 18. Mai 1948 anlässlich der 100-Jahrfeier der Deutschen Nationalversammlung wieder eingeweiht.

Wir überqueren die Berliner Straße und den Paulsplatz mit seinen Platanen. An der Braubachstraße, wo sich im historischen Salzhaus auf der rechten Ecke die Touristen-Information befindet, halten wir uns links. Nr. 35, die weitgehend originalgetreue Rekonstruktion des Steinernen Hauses von 1464, beherbergt heute den **Frankfurter Kunstverein**. An Gaststätten, Galerien, Läden sowie an dem Baugrundstück des ehemaligen Technischen Rathauses vorbei erreichen wir das **Museum für Moderne Kunst** von Hans Hollein. Der 1991 eröffnete Dreiecksbau, das so genannte ‚Tortenstück', besitzt eine herausragende zeitgenössische Kunstsammlung.

Wir laufen entlang der Domstraße und erreichen den gotischen **Dom**, in dessen Kreuzgang sich das **Dommuseum** befindet. Die katholische Bartholomäus-Kirche diente zwar nie als Bischofskirche, trägt aber die Bezeichnung ‚Kaiserdom'. Hier wurden seit 1356 Königswahlen abgehalten und später 10 Kaiser gekrönt. Der Dom erhielt mit den Restaurierungen ab 1948 sein heutiges Aussehen. Sehenswert sind im Inneren vor allem der hohe Chor und die Wahlkapelle.

Das südlich gelegene Leinwandhaus, das **Museum für Komische Kunst**, ist eines der wenigen gotischen Steinhäuser der Stadt. Das 1399 vollendete Gebäude diente neben dem Tuchhandel auch als Lazarett und Schlachthaus. 1984 wurde es wieder errichtet und 2007/08 zum Museum umgebaut.

Wir steigen die Treppe entlang den hellen Sandstein-Arkaden hinauf und erkennen rechts die 2. Front der Baustelle für das neue **Dom-Römer-Areal**. Auf 7.000 m² soll hier ein Teil der zerstörten Altstadt wieder entstehen. Dabei sind

afterwards at the Berliner Straße we turn left and the elliptical central building **Paulskirche** comes into view on the right. Built in 1833 as the main Evangelical Lutheran Church of the town it was soon used as the seat for the 1st all-German parliament because it had the largest and most modern hall in Frankfurt. In 1944 the sandstone structure was destroyed and on May, 18th 1948 on the occasion of the 100th anniversary of the German National Assembly inaugurated again. We cross the Berliner Straße and the Paulsplatz with its sycamore trees. At Braubachstrasse where the tourist information centre occupies the historical building, Salzhaus, on the right corner, we bear left. No.35, which is a close reconstruction of the original 'Steinerne Haus' from 1464, now houses **Frankfurt's Arts' Association**. We pass by restaurants, galleries, shops as well as the building plot of the former Technical Town hall and arrive at the **Museum of Modern Art** by Hans Hollein. The triangular building, which was opened in 1991, has an outstanding collection of contemporary art.

We walk along the Domstraße and reach the **Gothic Cathedral**, whose cloister is the home of the **Cathedral Museum**. The St. Bartholomews Church never served as an Episcopal church yet it was named **'Kaiserdom'** (emperors' cathedral). Since 1356 this was the place were kings were elected and the coronations of 10 emperors took place here. The cathedral has had its current appearance since the restoration of 1948. The choir and the electors' chapel are well worth visiting.

The 'Leinwandhaus' to the south of the cathedral houses the **Museum of Comic Art** and is one of the few Gothic stone buildings in the city. The building was completed in 1399, it was used in the cloth trade and in the past has served as a military hospital and even as a slaughterhouse.

Helvetia office building:

Characteristic, tip

In this building, for the first time in Frankfurt, thermo active *component activation* (concrete floor) was used. This ensures a pleasantly cool climate in summer and a comfortably warm one in winter – 1/3 created through the floor and 2/3 through the ceiling. A separate control system was developed, which takes into account the capacity of the system and its self-regulating effect.

Today Paulskirche is above all a place of remembrance for the beginning of German democracy. In the upper meeting room, for example, the International High-rise Award and the Goethe Prize of Frankfurt are awarded.

The east-west tram line, the so-called, 'Altstadtstrecke' (Old Town Line), is still in operation today. The tourist attraction, 'Ebbelwei-Express' (Cider-Express), runs on this route.

> Der 95 m hohe Turm des **Kaiserdoms** kann von April bis Oktober bestiegen werden. Nach 324 Stufen bietet sich dem Besucher ein herrliches Panorama über Frankfurt und die Rhein-Main-Region.

> In 2011 wurden die Ergebnisse des Wettbewerbs für den Wiederaufbau der Frankfurter Altstadt zwischen Römerberg und Dom verkündet. Eine 3D-Animation der neuen Frankfurter Altstadt finden Sie unter: www.domroemer.de
> Dort können Sie auch an einem virtuellen Rundgang mit frei schwenkbaren 360° Panoramen teilnehmen.

> Ein Besuch des Kaisersaals im ‚**Römer**' lohnt sich: In einem Gemäldezyklus sind hier alle 52 deutschen Herrscher verewigt. Das Gebäude kann auch virtuell in 3D-Panoramen besucht werden. Nähere Informationen unter: www.tinyurl.com/bxmnmq3

mindestens acht Rekonstruktionen und rund 20 Neubauten geplant. Alle unterliegen strengen Gestaltungsgrundsätzen, haben die aktuellen Bauanforderungen zu erfüllen und sollen möglichst nahe an den *Passivhaus*standard herankommen.

Wir durchqueren die Rotunde mit dem Eingang zur 1986 eröffneten, national und international renommierten **Schirn Kunsthalle**. Ihr Name erinnert an die einst hier vorhandenen offenen Verkaufsläden (Schirnen) der Frankfurter Metzger. Geradeaus gelangen wir auf den Römerberg und sehen rechts die Treppengiebel-Fassade des **Rathauses** mit ihren neugotischen Dekorationen. Das mittlere der ursprünglich drei eigenständigen Gebäude ist das eigentliche Haus ‚Zum Römer'. Hier wird seit 1405 Politik gemacht.

Auf dem Römerberg, ehemals Samstagsberg, fanden seit dem 9. Jahrhundert unter anderem Märkte und Messen, Turniere und Feste statt. Im 16. Jahrhundert galt Frankfurts ‚Gut' Stubb' als schönster Platz im Heiligen Römischen Reich. In seiner Mitte steht der Gerechtigkeitsbrunnen von 1611 mit seiner bronzenen Justitia-Statue von 1887. Im Gegensatz zu ihren üblichen Darstellungen sind ihre Augen nicht verbunden.

Der östliche Platz wird von den 1986 nach historischen Plänen erbauten **Fachwerkhäusern**

‚Römer', Rathaus/Town hall

In 1984 it was rebuilt and in 2007/08 transformed into a museum.

We go up the steps and walk along the light sandstone arcades. On the right we see the 2nd building site for the new **Dom-Römer-Areal** (cathedral-Römer area). On this 7,000m² area, part of the destroyed old town will be rebuilt. At least eight reconstructions and about 20 new buildings are planned. They are subject to design principles that have to adhere to current building requirements and, as far as possible, should be *Passive Houses*.

We pass through the rotunda with the entrance to the **Schirn Kunsthalle** which was opened 1986 and is nationally and internationally renowned. The name comes from Frankfurt's butchers' stalls (Schirnen) which were here in older times. Straight ahead of us is the Römerberg (Roman Hill), here we see to the right the stepped gable facade of the **Town Hall**, with its neo-Gothic decorations. The middle of the originally three separate buildings is the actual house 'Zum Römer'. It has been a venue for political discussions since 1405.

Markets and fairs, tournaments and festivals have been held on the Römerberg, formerly Samstagsberg (Saturday Hill), since the 9th Century. In the 16th century Frankfurt's 'Gut' Stubb' (parlour) was considered the most beautiful square in the Holy Roman Empire. In its centre is the Fountain of Justice, dated 1611, with its bronze statue of Justitia from 1887. Unlike its usual representations here the eyes are not blindfolded.

On the Eastern side of the square **half-timbered houses** were reconstructed in 1986 from historical plans, but unlike the original houses the wooden beams here have not been plastered over. On the right is the **old Church of St. Nicholas**. From the 13th to the 14th Century

Kaiserdom

The 95m high tower of the Kaiserdom can be visited from April to October. After the climb of 324 steps, a panoramic view of Frankfurt and the Rhine-Main region awaits the visitor.

The reconstruction of the old town of Frankfurt between Römerberg and Dom was open to competition and the results announced in 2011. For a 3D animation of the new Frankfurt's old town, visit: www.domroemer.de. There you can also see a 360° panoramic virtual tour.

> Das Energiemanagement für Gebäude wie Römer, Museen, Paulskirche und Städtische Bühnen übernimmt seit 1991 eine gleichnamige Abteilung des Hochbauamts der Stadt Frankfurt. Durch Controlling, Betriebsoptimierung und investive Maßnahmen (wie Leitlinien zum wirtschaftlichen Bauen) werden die Energie- und Wasserkosten für die etwa 1.000 städtisch genutzten Liegenschaften minimiert und die Klimaschutzziele des Magistrats umgesetzt. Der Verbrauch von Strom sank bis 2011 um rund 5%, von Heizenergie um 31%, von Wasser um 55%. Die die CO_2-Emissionen verringerten sich um 26%. Die Einsparungen belaufen sich seit 1990 auf über 100 Mio. €.
> Nähere Informationen unter: www.energiemanagement.stadt-frankfurt.de

bestimmt, die – entgegen der Originale – unverputzt blieben. Rechts befindet sich die **Alte Nikolaikirche**. Der doppelschiffige Hallenbau aus der Frühgotik war vom 13. bis 14. Jahrhundert kaiserliche Hofkapelle. Hörenswert ist das tägliche Glockenspiel um 9.00 und 12.00 Uhr. Wir lassen die Kirche links von uns und laufen nach Süden. Am Fahrtor entdecken wir das um 1600 erbaute Haus Wertheym, das als einziges Fachwerk der Altstadt den Bombenangriff von 1944 unversehrt überstand. Ihm gegenüber wird der Betonbau des **Historischen Museums** durch einen Neubau ersetzt. Er entsteht auf dem Gelände des Saalhofs: Die im 12. Jahrhundert errichtete Reichsburg löste die Kaiserpfalz auf dem Domhügel ab. Ihre zum Main hin gelegenen Gebäude wurden wiedererrichtet.

Wir lassen den **Eisernen Steg** links von uns und biegen an der **Leonhardskirche** rechts ab. Sie wurde 1219 als spätromanische Basilika erbaut, später gotisch gestaltet und besitzt wertvolle mittelalterliche Glasgemäldefenster. Geradeaus gelangen wir zu einem neuen, weiß verputzten Beratungs- und Verwaltungsgebäude, das gut in die Umgebung passt. Zusammen mit dem rechts dahinter liegenden Lebenshaus mit 25 Wohn-, 36 Pflegeeinheiten und gemeinschaftlich genutzten Veranstaltungsräumen sowie einer Kita bildet es das **Caritas Quartier**, Alte Mainzer Gasse 10. Die Blockrandbebauung von 2012 gruppiert sich um einen vom Leonhardskirchhof aus zugänglichen, halböffentlichen Innenhof mit denkmalgeschütztem Renaissance-Treppenturm. Das Bürogebäude sowie die Kita sind *Passivhäuser*. Ihre Belüftung und Beheizung erfolgen über die Lüftungsanlage, Wärmegewinnung und sommerliche Kühlung über ein Geothermiefeld im Innenhof. Regenwasser dient der Toilettenspülung. Das Lebenshaus erfüllt – ausgestattet mit Gas-Brennwertkessel mit

> Am Mainkai, Standort des ältesten Hafens der Stadt, legen auch heute noch Schiffe an. Sie bieten Ausflugsfahrten auf Main und Rhein an.

City | 5

‚Römer', Fachwerkhäuser/Half-timbered houses

A visit to the Imperial Hall in the 'Römer' is well worth it: In a series of paintings all 52 German rulers are commemorated here. This building can also be visited virtually with 3D panoramas at: www.tinyurl.com/bxmnmq3

the early Gothic hall-type construction with a double nave was the Imperial Court Chapel. It is worth listening to the daily carillon at 9.00 am and 12.00 pm. We leave the church on our left and walk in a southerly direction. At Fahrtor (position of an earlier gate between river Main & Römerberg) we discover the Wertheym house which was built around 1600 and is the only half-timbered house of the old town which survived the bombing of 1944 unscathed. Opposite the concrete building of the **Historical Museum** will soon be replaced by a new building on the site of the Saalhof: the imperial palace from the 12th Century. The imperials buildings overlooking the river Main have already been rebuilt.

We leave the **Eiserne Steg** (Iron Bridge) to our left and turn right at **Leonard's Church**. It was built in 1219 as a late Romanesque basilica and later decorated in Gothic style. It has valuable medieval stained glass windows. Moving straight ahead we arrive at a new whitewashed advice and administration building that fits well into the surroundings. It is the **Caritas Quartier** at No. 10 Alte Mainzer Gasse. It contains with the 'House of Life' 25 residential units, 36 care units and social rooms, as well as a Children's day care centre. The perimeter block from 2012 is grouped around a semi-public courtyard with

Since 1991 the energy management for buildings such as the Römer, the museums, St. Paul's Church and the City Theatre has been run by the energy management section of the Building Department of the City of Frankfurt. By controlling, optimizing operations and investment measures (such as guidelines for economic construction), the energy and water costs for about 1,000 urban used properties can be minimized by implementing the climate protection goals of the urban administration. Up to 2011 the consumption of electricity fell by around 5%, heating energy by 31% and water consumption by 55%. The CO_2 emissions were reduced by 26% and the costs sank by more than € 100 million. For more information:
www.energiemanagement.stadt-frankfurt.de

Der Caritasverband Frankfurt e.V. ist Mitglied beim 2010 gegründeten Verein ‚Energiepunkt – Energieberatungszentrum Frankfurt am Main'. Er ging aus einer Initiative des Umweltdezernats hervor und ist ein unabhängiger Wegweiser bei Energie- und Klimaschutzfragen. Nähere Informationen unter:
www.energiepunkt-frankfurt.de

Daneben fördern das Sozialdezernat und das Energiereferat der Stadt Frankfurt den ‚Cariteam-Energiesparservice': Beratungen für einkommensschwache Haushalte und Qualifizierung von Langzeitarbeitslosen zu Energie-Serviceberatern.

Caritas Quartier

Blockheizkraftwerk – die Kriterien der *EnEV* 2007. Wir folgen der Alten Mainzer Gasse entlang des Beratungs- und Verwaltungshauses nach Westen und erreichen das **Archäologische Museum**. Zusammen mit dem Institut für Stadtgeschichte befindet es sich im 1955 im spätgotischen Stil wieder aufgebauten Karmeliterkloster sowie in Bauten (1988) von Josef Paul Kleihues. Im Kreuzgang und Refektorium sind Renaissance-Fresken von Jörg Ratgeb zur Heilsgeschichte und zur Geschichte des Karmeliterordens zu sehen. Wir gehen die Alte Mainzer Gasse bis an ihr Ende. Dort hat sich links zum Main hin eine kleine Pforte der Stadtbefestigung von 1333 erhalten. Wir kommen am Kabarett ‚Die Schmiere' vorbei, überqueren an der nächsten Kreuzung die Hauptverkehrsader und folgen der Weißfrauenstraße nach links. Dabei passieren wir die Baustelle für das **Maintor Quartier.** Es soll das Bankenviertel mit Büro-, Wohn-, Einzelhandels- und Gastronomie-Bauten nach neuesten Green-Building-Standards komplettieren. Wir gehen geradeaus und erreichen den Willy-Brandt-Platz. Rechts steht das Hochhaus der Europäischen Zentralbank, links die 1963 eingeweihte und inzwischen umgebaute Theater-Doppelanlage der renommierten Städtischen Bühnen mit Schauspiel und Oper.

a listed Renaissance staircase tower which is accessible from the Leonard's churchyard. The office building and the day care centre are *passive houses*. Ventilation and heating is provided by a ventilation system and a geothermal field in the courtyard provides more heat and cooling as required. Rainwater is used for flushing the toilets. The House of Life – equipped with a gas condensing boiler with *CHP* – meets the criteria of *EnEV* 2007.

We follow Alte Mainzer Gasse past the advice and administrative building to the west and reach the **Archaeological Museum**. This, as well as the Institute of City History, is now in the Carmelite monastery which was rebuilt in 1955 in the late Gothic style and in buildings (1988) by Josef Paul Kleihues. In the cloister and the refectory renaissance frescoes by Jörg Ratgeb showing the history of salvation and the history of the Carmelite Order are to be seen. We follow the Alte Mainzer Gasse to its end where to the left towards the Main, a small gate from the city fortification from 1333 has been preserved. In the north we pass by the Cabaret, 'Die Schmiere', cross the road at the next junction and follow the main road Weißfrauenstraße to the left. Here we pass the construction site for the **Maintor Quartier**. It will complement the financial district with commercial, residential, retail and restaurant buildings according to the latest green building standards. We go straight on and arrive at Willy-Brandt-Platz. To the right we see the high-rise building of the European Central Bank and to the left the Municipal Theatre which was inaugurated in 1963 and has since been converted and now is renowned for both drama and opera.

Ships still dock on the Mainkai, site of the oldest port in the city. They offer trips on the rivers Main and Rhine.

The Association of the Caritas Frankfurt e.V. is a member of the club 'Energiepunkt' (Power point) – the Energy Advisory Centre Frankfurt founded in 2010. It emerged from an initiative of the Environment Department and is an independent guide on energy and climate issues. For more information:
www.energiepunkt-frankfurt.de

In addition, the welfare department and the Energy Department of the City of Frankfurt jointly promote 'Cariteam energy saving service': This offers counselling for low-income households and trains long-term unemployed to become energy service consultants.

Klimaschutzstadtplan:
Das Energiereferat und das Vermessungsamt der Stadt Frankfurt zeigen auf der Karte online, wo in Frankfurt *Blockheizkraftwerke,* Biomasse, *Photovoltaik,* Solarthermie, Wasser- und Windkraft zum Einsatz kommen. Auch städtische und andere Passiv- und Niedrigenergiebauten sind darin aufgeführt. Nähere Informationen unter:
www.klimaschutzstadtplan-frankfurt.de

Deutsche Börse:
Erstes Hochhaus in Deutschland mit LEED Platin-Zertifikat

Deutsche Börse:

Bauherr/Client
Lang & Groß Projektentwicklung GmbH

Architekt/Architect
KSP Jürgen Engel Architekten GmbH, Frankfurt am Main

Baujahr/Year of construction
2008–2010

Nutzfläche/Useful area
65.000 m²

Exkursionen
... mit der S3 oder S4

An der Station ‚Eschborn Süd' laufen wir entlang der Stuttgarter Straße bis zur Alfred-Herrhausen-Allee, biegen rechts ab und folgen ihr bis zum Kreisel mit der gelben Stahl-Skulptur ‚Fulcrum' von John Henry von 2001. Links vor uns sehen wir die Glasfassaden des Bundesamts für Wirtschaft und Ausfuhrkontrolle, das Aufgaben zum Erreichen der deutschen Klimaschutzziele übernimmt. Wir gehen geradeaus auf unser Ziel in der Eschborner Mergenthalerallee Nr. 61 zu.

Das 21-stöckige Gebäude der **Konzernzentrale der Deutschen Börse**, ‚The Cube', besteht aus zwei L-förmigen Türmen, die über 11 Stege und acht Brücken miteinander verbunden und komplett von einer Glasfassade umhüllt sind. Das 80 m hohe Foyer bildet das Herz des Neubaus,

Konzernzentrale/Headquarters Deutsche Börse

Konzernzentrale/Headquarters Deutsche Börse

Excursions
... with the S3 or S4

At the station 'Eschborn Süd' we walk along Stuttgarter Straße up to Alfred-Herrhausen-Allee, turn right and follow it to the roundabout with the yellow steel sculpture, 'Fulcrum', by John Henry from 2001. Straight ahead and to the left we see the glass facade of the Federal Office of Economics and Export Control whose aim is to attain the German climate protection goals. We then go straight on to our destination in Eschborner Mergenthalerallee No. 61.

The **Headquarters of Deutsche Börse** (German Stock Exchange) is a 21-storey building 'The Cube' composed of two L-shaped towers, which are connected to each other via 11 catwalks and eight bridges enclosed by a glass facade. The 80 meter high lobby is the heart of the new building and is a place of communication and staging of events. Photographs from the Art Collection 'Deutsche Börse' lend an individual flair to the whole arena. The integrated energy concept of the compact building structure combines creative, constructive and in-house

> **Climate Protection City Plan:**
> Frankfurts power stations can be found on an online map as well as information about *Passive Houses* and other energy efficient buildings under:
> www.klimaschutzstadt-plan-frankfurt.de

> **Deutsche Börse:**
> First skyscraper in Germany with LEED Platinum Certification

6 | Exkursionen

Deutsche Börse:

Energetisches Niveau
- *LEED*-Zertifikat in Platin 2010 für Bürohochhaus, Neubau
- Die gesetzlichen Anforderungen der *EnEV* 2009 werden um 50% unterschritten, voraussichtlich auch die der neuen *EnEV*.

Nutzung (erneuerbarer) Energien
- Einsatz von *Kraft-Wärme-Kopplung*, die mit Biogas CO_2-neutral betrieben werden kann
- Solarthermie für Warmwasser
- Lüftungsanlage mit *Wärmerückgewinnung*

Besonderheit, Tipp
Eine öffentlich zugängliche Kunstterrasse für verschiedene Ausstellungen. Seit Ende 2007 nimmt die Deutsche Börse an ‚ÖKOPROFIT', einer Aktion der Stadt Frankfurt für kleine und mittlere Unternehmen zum Einstieg ins Umweltmanagement, teil. Ziel ist, durch technische und organisatorische Maßnahmen sowie bewusstes Verhalten weniger Energie und Rohstoffe zu verbrauchen.

Ökohaus Arche:

Ein ungewöhnlicher Gewerbebau in Frankfurt

ist Ort der Kommunikation und Bühne für Veranstaltungen. Fotografien aus der Art Collection Deutsche Börse verleihen dem Ganzen ein individuelles Gesicht. Das integrative Energiekonzept des kompakten Baukörpers vereint gestalterische, konstruktive und haustechnische Maßnahmen und ermöglicht eine effiziente Nutzung: Die Büroflächen sind flexible Einheiten, deren raumhohe Fenster Tageslicht bis tief in das Innere fallen lassen. Zwei *Blockheizkraftwerke* decken rund 60% des Eigenstrombedarfs und dienen zum Heizen/Kühlen des Gebäudes mit einem jährlichen Primärenergieverbrauch von 150 kWh/m². Auch auf den Einsatz ressourcenschonender und umweltverträglicher Baustoffe wurde großer Wert gelegt. Als erstes Bürohochhaus in Deutschland erfüllt ‚The Cube' so den Platin-Standard des amerikanischen Klassifizierungssystems für ökologisches Bauen, *LEED*. Die Deutsche Börse engagiert sich darüber hinaus für Produkte und Dienstleistungen rund um eine nachhaltige Zukunft, wie Indizes zu Umweltthemen oder die Verminderung von CO_2-Emissionen.

... mit der S3 bis S6

Den Westbahnhof verlassen wir am Ausgang ‚Kasseler Straße'. Dort halten wir uns links und

Ökohaus Arche

technical measures and facilitates efficient use: The office spaces are flexible units with floor to ceiling windows that allow daylight to fall deep into the interiors. Two *CHP*s cover around 60% of the electricity requirements and have an annual primary energy consumption of 150 kWh/m² for heating/cooling the building. Great importance was attached to the use of resource-saving and environmentally-friendly building materials. Thus, the Cube is the first office tower in Germany to meet the platinum standard of the American classification system for sustainable building, *LEED*. The German Stock Exchange is also involved in dealing with products and services for a sustainable future such as indices of environmental issues and the reduction of CO_2 emissions.

... with the S3 to S6

We leave the Westbahnhof at 'Kasseler Straße' where we keep left and reach our goal after a few steps.

30 different users combined, ecology, building biology, economics and practicality in the building of **'Ökohaus Arche'** which was completed in 1992. Thus, the glass buildings, the green roof and the planted foyer with a stream play their part in the natural air conditioning;

Deutsche Börse:

Energetic level
| *LEED* Certificate 2010 for office building
| Legal requirements by *EnEV* 2009 were undercut by 50% as well as the expected requirements of the future *EnEV*.

Use (renewable) energy
| Use of *combined heat and power,* which can be powered CO_2-neutrally with biogas
| Solar heat for hot water
| Ventilation system with *heat recovery* system

Characteristic, tip
A publicly accessible art terrace for various exhibitions.
Since 2007 the German stock market has been taking part in 'ÖKO-PROFIT', a project of the City of Frankfurt for small and medium enterprises to participate in environmental management. The goal is to consume less energy and fewer ressources through technical and organizational measures and conscious behaviour.

Ökohaus Arche:

An unusual commercial building in Frankfurt

Ökohaus Arche

6 | Exkursionen

Müllheizkraftwerk Nordweststadt:

Zentrale Versorgung von Stadtteilen

Müllheizkraftwerk Nordweststadt:

Betreiber
Mainova AG

Strom- und Wärmeerzeugung
Seit 1967

Primärenergieträger
Haus- und Gewerbemüll (Siedlungsrückstände)

Erzeugungskapazität
Max. Strom 47 MW
Strom in *Kraft-Wärme-Kopplung* 37 MW
Fernwärme 167 MW

Versorgung mit Fernwärme
Nordweststadt, Riedberg, Uni-Campus, Hessischer Rundfunk, Polizeipräsidium

Fernheizmedium
Heizwasser

Besonderheit, Tipp
Kostenfreie, etwa zweistündige Führungen (Gruppen von 10–30 Personen) werden wochentags von 8.00–18.00 Uhr nach Voranmeldung angeboten:
Besucherdienst
der Mainova AG
Tel.: 069-213 27 945
E-Mail: fuehrungen@mainova.de
www.mainova.de

erreichen so bereits nach wenigen Schritten unser Ziel.

Das 1992 fertig gestellte Gebäude ,**Ökohaus Arche**' vereint auf Wunsch der über 30 verschiedenen Nutzer Ökologie, Baubiologie, Ökonomie und Alltagstauglichkeit. So dienen die Glasbauten, das begrünte Dach und das bepflanzte Foyer mit Bachlauf der natürlichen Klimatisierung, das Regenwasser zur Toilettenspülung und zur Bewässerung. Die Wärme aus der Abluft einer Druckerei wird in das Heizsystem des Hauses mit einem Energieverbrauch von rund 80 kWh/(m²a) eingespeist.

... mit der U1 oder U9

An der Haltestelle ,Heddernheimer Landstraße' lassen wir die Gleise rechts von uns und folgen dem Metallzaun des Werksgeländes bis zum Tor 1 unseres Ziels bei Nr. 157.

Die Nordweststadt entstand 1962 bis 1968 auf den Gemarkungen der Stadtteile Niederursel und Heddernheim. Die Planer entschieden sich für ein großes Heizkraftwerk und eine Abfallverbrennungsanlage. Denn bereits damals erschien *Fernwärme* als Alternative zu herkömmlichen Gasleitungen sinnvoll, zumal im Müll ein enormes Energie- und CO_2-Reduktions-Potenzial steckt. Seit 1967 wird bei der Abfallverbren-

Müllheizkraftwerk (MHKW) Nordweststadt

Excursions | 6

Müllheizkraftwerk (MHKW) Nordweststadt

rain water is used for toilet flushing and irrigation. The waste heat from a printing press is fed into the heating system of the building with an energy consumption of about 80 kWh/(m^2a).

... with the U1 or U9

At the subway stop 'Heddernheimer Landstraße' we leave the tracks to our right and follow the metal fence of the plant site to gate No. 1 of our goal at No. 157.

The Nordweststadt grew from 1962 to 1968 in the districts of Niederursel and Heddernheim. The designers opted for a large power plant and a waste incineration plant as even then heat from a *district heating* network made sense as an alternative to conventional gas pipelines, especially as there was a huge reduction potential of energy and CO_2 in waste material. Since 1967 both electricity and heat is produced during waste incineration, from which the power plant benefits. After extensive renovation work after 1st January 2007 the two plants were combined and are now a **Waste-To-Energy plant** (WTE), a plant network, whose processes are centrally monitored and controlled by computer. Since 2009, each year 525,000 tons of waste are burned to produce useful energy.

Müllheizkraftwerk Nordweststadt:

Central energy supply for city districts

Müllheizkraftwerk Nordweststadt:

Operator
Mainova AG

Power and heat production
Since 1967

Main energy producers
Household and commercial waste

Production capacity
Max. 47 MW electricity
Combined power and heat production of 37 MW
District heating 167 MW

Supplied by district heating
Nordweststadt, Riedberg, Uni-Campus, Hessischer Rundfunk (Hessian Broadcasting Corporation), Police headquarters

District heating
Heated water

Michael-Grzimek-Schule:

Campus mit Identifikationscharakter für Stadtteil Nieder-Eschbach

Michael-Grzimek-Schule:

Bauherr / Client
Stadt/City of Frankfurt a. Main, Stadtschulamt vertreten durch das Hochbauamt/Municipal education authority represented by the Construction Department

Architekt / Architect
Juri Troy Architects, Wien, gemeinsam mit/together with DI Matthias Hein und Kavan Architekten Frankfurt am Main

Baujahr / Year of construction
2008–2009

Nutzfläche/Useful area
2.800 m²

Energetisches Niveau
| *EnEV* (2007) -30%
| Auszeichnung als ‚*Green Building Frankfurt RheinMain*' in 2011

Nutzung (erneuerbarer) Energien
| Natürliche Lüftung und Beleuchtung
| Aktivierung der Betondecken als Speichermasse

Michael-Grzimek-Schule/School

nung sowohl Strom als auch Wärme produziert, von der das Heizkraftwerk profitiert. Nach umfangreichen Sanierungsarbeiten bilden die beiden ab dem 1. Januar 2007 als **Müllheizkraftwerk** (MHKW) einen Anlagenverbund, dessen Prozesse zentral computerunterstützt überwacht und gesteuert werden. Seit 2009 können jährlich 525.000 t Müll zu nutzbarer Energie verbrannt werden. Dies spart umgerechnet 175.000 t Steinkohle ein und sorgt für eine gute Umweltbilanz. Zu dieser trägt auch bei, dass Rückstände, wie Glas und Metalle, in einer Aufbereitungsanlage abgetrennt und weiterverwendet werden. Das Rauchgas wird von Schadstoffen und Staub gereinigt. Durch die ausgeklügelte Verfahrenstechnik ist das **MHKW Nordweststadt** eine der modernsten Anlagen Deutschlands. Ihr Betreiber, die Mainova AG, entstand 1998 aus der Stadtwerke GmbH und der Maingas AG.

… mit der U2 oder U9

An der Station ‚Nieder-Eschbach' orientieren wir uns zum Parkplatz in der Prager Straße. Dieser folgen wir, bis sie einen Versatz macht. Dabei haben wir unser Ziel bereits rechts von uns. Wir umrunden es und gelangen so zur Prager Straße zurück.

Excursions | 6

Michael-Grzimek-Schule/School

This saves the equivalent of 175,000 tons of coal and provides a good environmental balance. In addition, residues such as glass and metals are separated in a treatment plant and reused. The burnt gas is cleaned of pollutants and dust. Due to the sophisticated technology process, **MHKW Nordweststadt** is one of the most modern plants in Germany. Its operator, Mainova AG emerged in 1998 from the Stadtwerke GmbH and Main Gas AG.

... with the U2 or U9

At the station 'Nieder-Eschbach' we go to the parking lot in the Prager Straße. We follow this until the bend. We already have our goal on the right. We go around it and thus come back to Prager Straße.

The revitalization of the **Michael-Grzimek-School**, established in 1953, resulted in a new two-storey reinforced concrete building of 18 classrooms clad in prefabricated, highly insulated wall panels with an exterior facade encased in vertical larch wood. Sustainable effects are achieved because the shell of the previous building remains as a guiding theme of the extension. For the interior quality robust and easy-care materials were used. The main entrance, the library and the kiosk are the

Michael-Grzimek-School:

Campus with own character for the district of Nieder-Eschbach

Michael-Grzimek-School:

Energetic level
| EnEV (2007) -30%
| Awarded as 'Green Building Frankfurt' in 2011

Use (renewable) energy
| Natural ventilation and lighting
| Use of the concrete ceiling as mass storage

Characteristic, tip
| Use of durable, renewable and recyclable materials
| Double-sided lighting and ventilation of classrooms during all seasons
| Master plan with preservation or demolition of existing buildings for total energy-optimized balance
| The school playground and the sports facilities are available during out of school hours for public use.

6 | Exkursionen

Michael-Grzimek-Schule:

Besonderheit, Tipp
| Verwendung langlebiger, nachwachsender und recyclebarer Baustoffe
| Beidseitige Belichtung und Belüftung der Klassenräume zu allen Jahreszeiten
| Masterplan mit Erhalt oder Abriss von bestehenden Bauten für energetisch optimale Gesamtbilanz
| Der Schulhof und die Sportanlage sind auch außerhalb der Schulzeiten für die Öffentlichkeit zugänglich.

Die Revitalisierung der 1953 errichteten **Michael-Grzimek-Schule** impliziert einen neuen zweigeschossigen Stahlbetonbau für 18 Klassenräume. Er ist mit vorgefertigten, hoch wärmegedämmten Wandelementen mit vertikaler Lärchenholzschalung verkleidet. Nachhaltig wirkt sich auch aus, dass der Rohbau des Vorgängergebäudes Bestandteil und Leitthema dieser Erweiterung ist. Für das Interieur wurden wertige, robuste und pflegeleichte Materialien eingesetzt. Herz der Anlage ist ein Verbindungstrakt mit Haupteingang, Mediathek und Kiosk. 2011 wurde der Campus durch eine Sporthalle samt -platz ergänzt. Die Schule hat viele flexibel nutzbare Flächen und wertet mit bepflanzten Außenbereichen das gesamte Quartier auf.

... mit der U3
Wir fahren bis zum ‚Kupferhammer', überqueren die Hohemarkstraße und folgen ihr – die U-Bahn links von uns – bis zur Camp-King-Allee. Diese laufen wir den Berg hinauf, dann geradeaus den Jean-Sauer-Weg, bis wir rechts in den Heinrich-Kappus-Weg einbiegen.

Graues Haus, Oberursel:

Reduktion auf das Wesentliche

Graues Haus, Oberursel:

Bauherr/Client
Sergio Cantón und Cornelia Thielen

Architekt/Architect
Cantón Thielen Architekten, Oberursel (Taunus) – Camp King Areal

Baujahr/Year of construction
2005–2006

Nutzfläche/Useful area
175 m²

Graues Haus, Oberursel

hub of the building. In 2011, the campus was complemented by a sports hall with a sports field. The school has many flexible usable spaces and is enhanced by landscaped outdoor areas over the entire site.

... with the U3

We take the subway to the station 'Kupferhammer', cross the Hohemarkstraße and follow the underground tracks on the left to Camp-King-Allee. We walk up the hill, then straight along Jean-Sauer-Weg and then turn right into Heinrich-Kappus-Weg.

Graues Haus, Oberursel

The **Graue Haus** (grey house) at No. 12 cleverly combines ecology and economy with high-quality design. The detached house built to the future-oriented *Passive House* standard is successful redensification in a settlement from the 1930s. The simple monochrome building fits into the surroundings of gabled, half-timbered houses by focusing in detail and material. Its prefabricated timber frame construction with cellulose insulation shows how sustainable construction can be implemented without major economic additional expenditure in a construction period of five months. The lean building technology concept creates a healthy indoor climate with high quality and low energy consumption.

We follow the road further, turn right into Edith-Stein-Weg and then we turn right into Ahornweg. We go down Hohemarkstraße, back to the subway station.

At the station 'Oberursel' we can transfer to the S5. The first German **energy-plus quarters** are due to be built opposite the S5 station 'Stierstadt' on Zimmersmühlenweg. On about 3 hectare of the former Hessen Glass company grounds, residential and commercial development is planned. The energy concept of

Graues Haus, Oberursel:

Reduction to the essentials

Graues Haus, Oberursel:

Energetic level
| *Passive House* awarded as:
'Green Building FrankfurtRheinMain' 2011
'Vorbildliche Bauten in Hessen 2008'/AKH
'Energieeffiziente Architektur in Deutschland' 2008/Wüstenrot Stiftung

Use (renewable) energy
| Geothermal energy
| Fresh air comfort heating
| Natural lighting

Graues Haus, Oberursel:

Energetisches Niveau
| *Passivhaus*
  mit Auszeichnungen:
  ‚*Green Building Frankfurt-RheinMain*' 2011
  ‚Vorbildliche Bauten in Hessen 2008'/AKH
  ‚Energieeffiziente Architektur in Deutschland' 2008/Wüstenrot Stiftung

Nutzung (erneuerbarer) Energien
| Geothermie
| Frischluft-Komfort-Heizung
| Natürliche Belichtung

Besonderheit, Tipp
| Einsatz von nachhaltigen sowie recycelbaren Baustoffen
| Hocheffiziente Lüftungsanlage als Frischluft- Komfortheizung (Kompaktaggregat mit Kleinst*wärmepumpe* für Brauchwasser und Zulufterwärmung) mit einer *Wärmerückgewinnung* von 85%. Die Luftvorerwärmung/ -kühlung erfolgt durch einen *Sole*-Erdwärme tauscher (*Sole*-Korb) in rund 3 m Bodentiefe.

Campo am Bornheimer Depot:

Nachverdichtung im Passivhausstandard

Das **Graue Haus** bei Nr. 12 vereint geschickt Ökologie und Ökonomie mit einer hochwertigen Gestaltung: Das freistehende Einfamilienhaus im zukunftsträchtigen *Passivhaus*standard ist eine gelungene Nachverdichtung in einer Siedlung der 1930er Jahre. Dabei übersetzt der schlichte monochrome Baukörper die giebelständigen Fachwerkhäuser der Umgebung zeitgemäß und setzt durch wenige Details und Materialen Akzente. Seine vorgefertigte Holzständerbauweise mit Zellulosedämmung zeigt, wie nachhaltiges Bauen ohne größeren wirtschaftlichen Mehraufwand in einer Bauzeit von fünf Monaten realisiert werden kann. Das schlanke Haustechnikkonzept schafft ein gesundes Raumklima mit hoher Lebensqualität und geringem Energieverbrauch.

Wir folgen der Straße, dann rechts dem Edith-Stein-Weg, von wo aus wir rechts zum Ahornweg abbiegen. Wir gehen bergab zur Hohemarkstraße, zurück zur U-Bahn-Station.

Am Bahnhof ‚Oberursel' können wir zur S5 umsteigen. Gegenüber der S5-Bahnstation ‚Stierstadt' soll am Zimmersmühlenweg das erste deutsche **Plus-Energie-Quartier** entstehen. Auf dem rund 3 ha großen Gelände der einstigen Hessen-Glas sind Wohn- und Gewerbenutzung geplant. Das Energiekonzept des Quartiers wird darauf abgestimmt, insgesamt mehr Energie zu erzeugen als zu verbrauchen. Nähere Informationen zu dem vom Bundeswirtschaftsministerium geförderten, zweijährigen Forschungsprojekt unter: www.ee.architektur.tu-darmstadt.de

... mit der U4 oder Tram 12

An der Haltestelle ‚Bornheim Mitte' orientieren wir uns zur Ecke Berger Straße/Saalburgstraße. Letzterer folgen wir links nach Nordwesten, an der Straßenbahnstation vorbei. An der nächsten

Excursions | 6

the neighbourhood is tuned to produce more energy than it consumes. For more information on the Federal Economics Ministry funded two-year research project: www.ee.architektur.tu-darmstadt.de

... with the U4 or Tram 12

At the stop 'Bornheim Mitte' we go to the corner Berger Straße/Saalburgstraße where turning left we continue in a north westerly direction past the tram station. At the next junction we turn right into Heidestraße.

With the **Campo in Frankfurt-Bornheim** a new district centre was developed. It has 160 apartments of the *Passive House* standard, a supermarket, retail shops and a bistro. The ensemble was, at its completion, the largest urban *Passive House* residential district of Germany. The four- and five-storey building blocks have various floor plans. Despite the dense development, the courtyards of the 11 town houses offer attractive outdoor areas. The listed buildings of the area were mostly preserved and

Graues Haus, Oberursel,

Characteristic, tip
| Use of sustainable and recyclable materials
| Highly efficient ventilation system realized by fresh air comfort heating (compact unit with small *heat pump* for domestic hot water and heating air) with *heat recovery* of 85%. The air preheating/cooling is provided by a *brine* ground heat exchanger (brine-basket) at a depth of 3m.

Campo in Bornheim:

Redensification to the Passive House standard

Campo in Bornheim

**Campo
am Bornheimer Depot:**

Bauherr/Client
ABG Frankfurt Holding GmbH

Architekt/Architect
Albert Speer & Partner GmbH – Architekten, Scheffler + Partner Architekten, Stefan Forster Architekten – Frankfurt am Main, Hoechstetter und Partner Architekten – Darmstadt

Baujahr/Year of constr.
2006–2009

Nutzfläche/Useful area
14.000 m²

Energetisches Niveau
| *Passivhäuser*
| Auszeichnung als ‚Green Building Frankfurt-RheinMain' in 2011

Nutzung (erneuerbarer) Energien
| Abwärme der Kleinkälteanlagen des Supermarkts sorgt für Warmwasseraufbereitung der Wohnungen
| Individuell regelbare Lüftungsanlagen mit *Wärmerückgewinnung*

Besonderheit, Tipp
| Hochwärmegedämmte Außenelemente, aus möglichst natürlichen und recycelbaren Materialien
| Heizkosten von rund 5 €/Monat für 100 m² Wohnung – 75% geringere Energiekosten im Vergleich mit anderen Neubauten

Kreuzung biegen wir rechts in die Heidestraße ab.
Mit dem **Campo in Frankfurt-Bornheim** entstand links ein neues Stadtteilzentrum mit 160 *Passivhaus*wohnungen, einem Supermarkt, Einzelhandelsgeschäften und einem Bistro. Das Ensemble war bei seiner Fertigstellung das größte innerstädtische *Passivhaus*-Wohnquartier Deutschlands. Die vier- und fünfgeschossigen Gebäuderiegel weisen vielfältige Grundrisse auf. Trotz der dichten Bebauung bieten die Innenhöfe der 11 Stadthäuser attraktive Aufenthaltsbereiche. Die denkmalgeschützten Bauten des Areals wurden weitgehend erhalten und saniert. Sie bewahren den ursprünglichen Charakter des ehemaligen Straßenbahndepots. Ein öffentlicher Fußweg verbindet nun die Heidestraße mit der Gronauer Straße.
Wir schlendern die Heidestraße entlang. Am Fünffingerplätzchen wenden wir uns scharf nach rechts und laufen die **Berger Straße**, Frankfurts längste Einkaufsstraße, bis zum Bornheimer Marktplatz mit einem roten Sandsteinbrunnen und Uhrtürmchen.
Wir biegen rechts in die Wiesenstraße ab und folgen später dem Anstieg der Hartmann-Ibach-Straße, bis sie auf die Butzbacher Straße trifft. Unterwegs fällt uns rechts der Eingang zum

Rotlintstraße 116–128

restored and still have the original character of the former tram depot. A public walkway connects Heidestraße with Gronauer Straße.

We stroll along Heidestraße. At Fünffingerplätzchen we take a sharp turn to the right and go along **Berger Straße**, Frankfurt's longest shopping street, until we reach the Bornheimer marketplace with a red sand stone fountain and small clock tower.

We turn right into Wiesenstraße and then follow Hartmann-Ibach-Straße uphill until it meets Butzbacher Straße. On the way we see the entrance to **Günthersburg Park** on the right. At the Butzbacher Straße we bear left and see, on the right, the red wall of our goal. Since 2007 the three **apartment blocks in 116–128 Rotlintstraße** have been gradually renovated to *Passive House* standard. The 1950s buildings will have prefabricated wooden parts and cellulose as wall insulation and a rapeseed oil-fired *CHP* unit will also be installed. Thermal solar panels on the roofs also support the hot water requirements. The heating requirement of the 56 apartments dropped from 200 to 15 kWh/ (m²a). The State of Hesse subsidised the CO_2-reducing project. We go back the way we came. From **Günthersburg Park** we can take the tram No. 12.

... with the U4 or U7

At the station 'Schäfflestraße' we pass through a gatehouse with red-brick plaster and arrive at the **Riederwald settlement** from the 1920s. We follow the avenue of sycamore trees to Lassallestraße. There, to the right we reach Engelsplatz. Here we go diagonally to the left through another gatehouse and go via a pedestrian and bicycle path to **Max-Hirsch-Straße 49–59**. In 2010, this row of shops was renewed in a comprehensive energy refurbishment (to *EnEV* 2009 standards) and

---

Campo
in Bornheim:

Energetic level
| *Passive Houses*
| Awarded as *'Green Building Frankfurt RheinMain'* in 2011

Use (renewable) energy
| Waste heat from the small refrigeration systems of the supermarket provides hot water in all apartments
| Individually adjustable ventilation systems with *heat recovery*

Characteristic, tip
| High-insulation exterior elements preferably made of natural and recyclable materials
| The residents in a 100m² apartment have heating costs of about €5 a month. This is about 75% lower energy costs in comparison to other new buildings.

> Links vom Marktplatz liegt der ‚SchubLaden' mit umweltfreundlichen Produkten. Wenn Sie in dem Ausbildungsprojekt etwas einkaufen, erhalten Sie bei Vorlage dieses Reiseführers einen kostenfreien Kaffee, Cappuccino oder Latte Macchiato.
> Spessartstrasse 11
> Tel.: 0 69 - 46 00 36 04
> Mo–Fr 9.30–18.30 Uhr
> Sa 10.00–14.00 Uhr

Günthersburgpark auf. An der Butzbacher Straße halten wir uns links und sehen rechts die rote Querwand unseres Ziels: Die drei **Wohnblocks in der Rotlintstraße 116–128** wurden seit 2007 auf *Passivhaus*standard saniert. Bei den Gebäuden aus den 1950er Jahren kommen erstmals Holz-Fertigteile und Zellulose als Fassadendämmung sowie ein mit Rapsöl befeuertes *Blockheizkraftwerk* zum Einsatz. Thermische Solarkollektoren auf den Dächern unterstützen zusätzlich die Warmwasserbereitung. Der Heizwärmebedarf der 56 Wohnungen sank von 200 auf 15 kWh/(m²a). Das Land Hessen förderte das CO_2-reduzierende Projekt. Wir laufen so zurück, wie wir gekommen sind. Ab dem **Günthersburgpark** können wir die Tram 12 nehmen.

... mit der U4 oder U7

An der Station ‚Schäfflestraße' gelangen wir durch ein ziegelrot verputztes Torhaus in die **Riederwaldsiedlung** aus den 1920er Jahren. Wir folgen der Platanen-Allee bis zur Lassallestraße. Dort nach rechts erreichen wir den Engelsplatz. Hier gehen wir schräg links durch ein weiteres Gebäudetor und kommen auf einem Fuß- und Radweg zur **Max-Hirsch-Straße 49–59**. Die ‚**Ladenzeile**' wurde 2010 im Rahmen einer umfassenden Kernsanierung energetisch (Neubaustandard *EnEV* 2009) und denkmalgerecht erneuert: Für die Außenwände, die sich um nicht mehr als 7 cm verbreitern durften, wurden hoch dämmende Hartschaum-Platten eingesetzt. Dreifach verglaste Fenster, dezentrale Lüftungsanlagen und moderne Heizungstechnik schaffen ein angenehmes Wohnklima. Die Originalfassade wurde nachgebildet, der Farbanstrich aus der Entstehungszeit des westlichen Quartiers rekonstruiert.

Gegenüber erinnert am ehemaligen Wohngebäude von Johanna Tesch eine Gedenktafel an

> Die Dachkonstruktion der Ladenzeile wurde etwas verlängert, die gemauerten Steinbänke und der Klinker am Sockel reproduziert. Grundrissänderungen unter Einbeziehung der ursprünglichen Mansarden brachten Platz für moderne Familienwohnungen. Die Stadt Frankfurt bezuschusste das Vorhaben mit 730.000 €.

> Mit dem Generalbebauungsplan für den Frankfurter Osten entwickelt sich ab 1909 ein Industrie- und Hafengebiet mit Wohnsiedlungen. Für die dort beschäftigten Arbeiter baute der 1900 gegründete Volks-Bau- und Sparverein von 1908–1914 die so genannte ‚Riederwald-Kolonie'. Ihre Straßen sind nach Persönlichkeiten der Reformbewegung benannt.

‚Ladenzeile' in der Max-Hirsch-Straße 49–59

renovated according to the guidelines for listed buildings. For the exterior walls, which could only be widened by a maximum of 7cm, highly insulating foam panels were used. Triple-glazed windows, central ventilation systems and advanced heating technology were installed to create a comfortable living environment. The original facade was reproduced and repainted according to the original construction of the western district.

Across the street at her former dwelling is a memorial tablet for Johanna Tesch, the Social Democrat who died in the Ravensbrück Concentration Camp in 1945. We follow the Max-Hirsch-Straße and breathe in the atmosphere of Frankfurt's first closed settlement with residential infrastructure and mostly historic buildings. The cooperative quarters from 1914 indicate, even today, a continuous construction and usage structure. The settlement plan and the layout of the groups of houses are based on the ideas of the 'Gartenstadtbewegung' (Garden City movement). The variety of detail and the yet overall homogeneous appearance are features which were worth protecting in the western region. We cross the Johanna-Tesch-Platz to arrive at the subway station of the same name.

On the left of the market place is the shop, 'SchubLaden', with environment-friendly products. When you shop in this vocational training project you will receive a free coffee, cappuccino or latte upon presentation of this guide.
Spessartstraße 11
Phone: 069-46 00 36 04
Mon–Fri 9.30 am–6.30 pm, Sat 10.00 am–2.00 pm

The roofs of this row of shops have been somewhat extended, the stone benches and the brick base reproduced. Changes to the plans which took the original mansards into account made place for modern family homes. The city of Frankfurt subsidized the project with € 730,000.

A port and industrial area with housing estates came into being in Frankfurt's eastern areas as a result of the general development plan from 1909. For the workers employed there, the 'Volks-Bau- und Sparverein' (People's Building and Savings Association), founded in 1900, built the so-called 'Riederwald colony' from 1908 to 1914. Its streets are named after personalities of the Reform Movement.

6 | Exkursionen

Staatliche Vogelschutzwarte:
Nachhaltiger Klima- und Naturschutz

Staatliche Vogelschutzwarte:

Bauherr/Client
Landesbetrieb Hessen-Forst

Architekt/Architect
anja thede architektur und farbgestaltung, Darmstadt

Baujahr/Year of construction
2009–2011

Nutzfläche/Useful area
270 m²

Energetisches Niveau
| EnEV 2009

Nutzung (erneuerbarer) Energien
| Einsatz nachwachsender, recyclebarer Materialien
| Holzpellet-Heizungssystem
| Natürliche Belichtung und Belüftung über Fensterflächen
| Ökologischer Vollwärmeschutz

die 1945 im KZ Ravensbrück gestorbene Sozialdemokratin. Wir genießen das Flair der ersten geschlossenen Wohnsiedlung Frankfurts mit wohnungsbezogener Infrastruktur und ihren meist historischen Bauten, indem wir der Max-Hirsch-Straße folgen. Das genossenschaftliche Quartier von 1914 kennzeichnet bis heute ein durchgängiges Bau- und Nutzungsgefüge. Der Siedlungsgrundriss und die Anlage der Häusergruppen orientieren sich an den Ideen der Gartenstadtbewegung. Das im Einzelnen vielfältige und insgesamt doch homogene Erscheinungsbild machen die schützenswerte Besonderheit des westlichen Gebiets aus. Wir überqueren den Johanna-Tesch-Platz und gelangen so zur gleichnamigen U-Bahnstation.

Wir fahren bis zur ‚Gwinnerstraße' und nehmen dort den Bus F-41 (Offenbach Hauptbahnhof) oder 44 (Friedhof Fechenheim). An der Haltestelle ‚Steinauer Straße' steigen wir aus und folgen dem Schild ‚**Vogelschutzwarte**' zum Haus Nr. 44.

Die Länder Hessen, Rheinland-Pfalz und Saarland betreiben gemeinsam mit der Stadt Frankfurt eine Vogelschutzwarte. Das Institut für angewandte Vogelkunde liegt am Rande des Fechenheimer Waldes. Die Nachkriegsgebäude wurden unter dem Aspekt ‚Vorbildlicher Klimaschutz' saniert und erhielten einen neuen Mitteltrakt. Der zweigeschossige Holzbau ist mit Holzfaserplatten gedämmt und mit einer farblich strukturierten Leistenschalung überzogen. Die große Glasschiebetür mit davorliegender Terrasse öffnet den Ausstellungsbereich nach außen. Im Inneren befinden sich auch Büro- und Besprechungsräume, die Bibliothek und ein Archiv. Das Hörsaalgebäude links davon wird vollflächig begrünt sein und so vielen Vögeln Lebensraum bieten können. Der Bau verfügt nun zudem über einen Vollwärmeschutz aus Zellulo-

Excursions | 6

Vogelschutzwarte/Bird conservation observatory

At the station 'Gwinnerstraße' we take the bus F-41 (Offenbach Hauptbahnhof) or 44 (Friedhof Fechenheim). At the bus stop 'Steinauer Straße' we get out and follow the signs to **'Vogelschutzwarte'** (Bird conservation observatory) to house No. 44.

The states of Hessen, Rheinland-Pfalz and Saarland jointly with city of Frankfurt run a Bird conservation observatory. The Institute for Applied Ornithology is on the edge of the Fechenheimer forest. The post-war buildings were renovated according to the vision of 'Exemplary Climate Protection' and a new middle section was added. The two-storey timber building is insulated with wood fibreboards and covered with a coloured, structured stripped casing. A large sliding glass door leads from the front terrace into the exhibition area. Inside there are offices and meeting rooms, the library and archives. The auditorium building on the left will have plants over the entire surface in order to provide a habitat for birds. The building is also fully thermally insulated with cellulose insulation which is mounted on a

Staatliche Vogelschutzwarte:

Sustainable climate and nature conservation

Staatliche Vogelschutzwarte:

Energetic level
| EnEV 2009

Use (renewable) energy
| Use of renewable, recyclable materials
| Wood pellet heating system
| Natural light and ventilation through windows
| Ecological complete thermal insulation

Characteristic, tip
The Institute is open to the public by prior appointment. The library includes more than 8,000 items, the Media Centre thousands of ornithological subjects. There are currently about 150 registered species in the feather collection (scientific reference collection). The slide (sample) collection contains about 1,000 bird exhibits. Events and course dates can be found under: www.vswffm.de

Staatliche Vogelschutzwarte:

Besonderheit, Tipp
Das Institut ist nach Voranmeldung öffentlich zugänglich. Die Bibliothek umfasst über 8.000 Titel, die Mediathek viele tausend ornithologische Motive. In der Federsammlung (wissenschaftliche Vergleichssammlung) sind derzeit etwa 150 Arten registriert. Rund 1.000 Vogelexponate enthält die Präparatesammlung. Veranstaltungs- und Kurstermine finden Sie unter: www.vswffm.de

sedämmung, der auf einer Putzträgerplatte aus Holzweichfaserplatte angebracht ist. Das rechte Seitengebäude mit der Verwaltung wurde äußerlich originalgetreu rekonstruiert. Sämtliche Maßnahmen führten zu einer Halbierung der Heizkosten und einer vorbildlichen CO_2-Bilanz. Das Motto „Staatliche Vogelschutzwarte – für Vögel und Menschen" zeigt sich auch bei den Fenstern: Sie sorgen für angenehm helle Innenräume. Gleichzeitig sind ihre speziellen Gläser sowie Beschichtungen für Vögel als Barriere sichtbar. Über 30 Vogelarten brüten auf dem Gelände, im Wald, im Garten und in speziellen Nisthilfen an den Gebäuden.

Wir gehen zurück auf die Birsteiner Straße und folgen ihr links durch das Wohngebiet nach Osten. Dann laufen wir rechts die Vilbeler Landstraße samt Unterführung, bis wir den Knotenpunkt ‚Mainkur' erreichen. Hier lassen wir den Hotel- und Casinobau auf der Verkehrsinsel rechts von uns und gelangen in die Straße ‚Alt Fechenheim'. Sie führt uns zum Eingang unseres nächsten Ziels bei Nr. 34 und zur Straßenbahnhaltestelle ‚Alt Fechenheim'.

Vogelschutzwarte/Bird conservation observatory

base board made of soft wooden fibreboard. The administration building on the right was reconstructed true to the original. All measures have led to a halving of the heating costs and an exemplary CO_2 balance. The motto, 'Bird conservation observatory – for birds and humans' is also realised by the windows, as they ensure a pleasant bright interior but can be seen by the birds due to special glass and coatings. More than 30 species of birds breed on the site, in the woods, in the garden and in special nesting boxes on the buildings.

We go back to Birsteiner Straße and continue towards the left through the residential area to the east. Then we go to the right along Vilbeler Landstraße through the underpass until we reach the intersection, 'Mainkur'. Here we leave the hotel and Casino buildings by the traffic island on our right and turn into the street, 'Alt Fechenheim'. It leads us to the entrance of our next target at No. 34 and to the tram stop 'Alt Fechenheim'.

The implementation of a climate protection strategy can be seen in Frankfurt even in its energy production: It focuses on power plants with exemplary environmental performance, such as the **biomass power plant in Fechenheim**. Since 2005 heat and electricity is obtained from about 100,000 tons of garden waste and recyclable wood annually. About 80,000 tons of this material is from Frankfurt. The system involves a CO_2 saving of around 85,000 tons per year since wood burns almost completely CO_2 neutrally: it releases only the amount that it has absorbed from the atmosphere during its growth. In addition, the chimney of the power station has a multi-stage burnt gas cleansing system so that even contaminated wood can be easily burned. Not only the fuel but also the customers are close by, resulting in overall

---

Biomasse-Kraftwerk Fechenheim:

Energy production with climate protection

Biomasse-Kraftwerk Fechenheim:

Operator
Mainova AG and WISA GmbH on the property of Allessa GmbH

Power and heat production
Since 2005

Main energy producers
Wood and green waste

Production capacity
Max. 12 MW electricity
Combined power and heat production of 7 MW
District heating 27 MW

Supplied by district heating
Industrial area of Allessa GmbH

District heating
Steam

6 | Exkursionen

Biomasse-Kraftwerk Fechenheim:

Energieerzeugung mit Klimaschutz

Biomasse-Kraftwerk Fechenheim:

Betreiber
Mainova AG und WISA GmbH auf dem Gelände der Allessa GmbH

Strom- und Wärmeerzeugung
Seit 2005

Primärenergieträger
Holz und Grünschnitt

Erzeugungskapazität
Max. Strom 12 MW
Strom in *Kraft-Wärme-Kopplung* 7 MW
Fernwärme 27 MW

Versorgung mit Fernwärme
Industriegelände der Allessa GmbH

Fernheizmedium
Dampf

Besonderheit, Tipp
Kostenfreie, etwa zweistündige Führungen (Gruppen von 10–30 Personen) werden wochentags von 8.00–18.00 Uhr nach Voranmeldung angeboten:
Besucherdienst der Mainova AG
Tel.: 069-213 27 945
E-Mail: fuehrungen@mainova.de
www.mainova.de

Biomasse-Kraftwerk/Biomass power plant Fechenheim

Die Umsetzung einer Klimaschutzstrategie zeigt sich in Frankfurt auch bei der Energieerzeugung: Sie setzt auf Anlagen mit vorbildlicher Umweltbilanz, wie das **Biomasse-Kraftwerk Fechenheim**. Seit 2005 wird hier Wärme und Strom aus rund 100.000 t Grünabfällen und Altholz pro Jahr gewonnen. Davon stammen rund 80.000 t aus Frankfurt und Umgebung. Das System bringt eine CO_2-Ersparnis von jährlich etwa 85.000 t mit sich, da Holz nahezu CO_2-neutral verbrennt: Es setzt nur die Menge frei, die es während seines Wachstums aus der Atmosphäre aufgenommen hat. Zudem verfügt der Schornstein des Kraftwerks über eine mehrstufige Rauchgasreinigung, so dass auch verunreinigtes Holz problemlos verfeuert werden kann. Aber nicht nur das Brennmaterial, sondern auch die Kunden sind in der Nähe, was insgesamt zu kurzen Transportwegen und einer ausgezeichneten Klimaschutzbilanz des Biomasse-Kraftwerks führt. Es erhielt deshalb auch besondere Beachtung, als die Stadt Frankfurt mit dem ‚Climate Star 2004' ausgezeichnet wurde. Die ausgekoppelte Wärme deckt den Bedarf von 8.000 Einfamilienhäusern, die erzeugte Strommenge reicht für 20.000 Haushalte.

Biomasse-Kraftwerk/Biomass power plant Fechenheim

short transport distances and an excellent climate balance of the biomass plant. For this is received special attention when the city of Frankfurt was awarded the 'Climate Star 2004'. The produced heat covers the needs of 8,000 single-family houses; the amount of electricity generated is enough for 20,000 homes.

... with the U6

At the station 'Friedhof Westhausen' we take the stairway down to Kollwitzstraße. We cross to the right, turn into Heinrich-Lübke-Straße, keep to the left and walk along it, parallel to the Ludwig-Landmann-Straße.

The comprehensive renovation of the **Heinrich-Lübke-Siedlung** (settlement) built in the 1970s, where about 2,000 people live in 600 subsidized apartments, is a model project for sustainable and economic renovation true to the 'Konzept der sozialverträglichen Mischung' (concept of a socially acceptable integration). With targeted interventions the quality of the existing buildings is to be strengthened, while modernizing its urban design, environmental and social aspects. New buildings to *Passive House* standards complement the existing structure. In particular it is important to achieve a higher quality of living and reduce

6 | Exkursionen

Heinrich-Lübke-Siedlung:

Leitbild für die Sanierung eines städtischen Großquartiers

Heinrich-Lübke-Siedlung:

Bauherr / Client
ABG Frankfurt Holding GmbH

Architekt / Architect
Albert Speer & Partner GmbH – Architekten, Jo. Franzke Architekten – Frankfurt am Main

Baujahr/Year of constr.
2010–2015

Nutzfläche/Useful area
90.000 m²

Energetisches Niveau
| Bestandsgebäude: Unterschreiten der *EnEV 2009* für Sanierungen um etwa 55%
| Neubauten Wohnen: *Passivhäuser*
| Gewerbeflächen: nach *EnEV*

Nutzung (erneuerbarer) Energien
| Anschluss an das Nahwärmenetz mit eigener Heizzentrale
| Dachflächen: Solarkollektoren, *Photovoltaik*
| Natürliche Belichtung und Belüftung
| Lüftungsanlage mit *Wärmerückgewinnung*

Heinrich-Lübke-Siedlung/Settlement

... mit der U6

Bei ‚Friedhof Westhausen' nehmen wir den Abgang zur Kollwitzstraße. Diese überqueren wir rechts, biegen in die Heinrich-Lübke-Straße ein, halten uns links und schlendern sie, parallel zur Ludwig-Landmann-Straße, entlang.

Die umfassende Erneuerung der in den 1970er Jahren gebauten **Heinrich-Lübke-Siedlung**, in der rund 2.000 Menschen in 600 geförderten Wohnungen leben, ist ein Modellprojekt für eine nachhaltige und wirtschaftliche Erneuerung nach dem ‚Konzept der sozialverträglichen Mischung'. Mit gezielten Eingriffen werden die Qualitäten der bestehenden Bebauung gestärkt und unter stadtgestalterischen, ökologischen und sozialen Aspekten modernisiert. Neubauten im *Passivhaus*standard ergänzen die bestehende Struktur. Insbesondere gilt es, eine höhere Wohnqualität und einen um über 90% geringeren CO_2-Ausstoß zu erzielen. Im Sommer des Jahres 2012 waren die Sanierungsarbeiten in den ersten Wohnhäusern des Quartiers in dem nordwestlichen Stadtteil Frankfurts abgeschlossen: Die Fassaden wurden gedämmt, die Fenster erneuert und vergrößert, die Bäder renoviert, Balkone angesetzt und Eingänge freundlicher gestaltet, um sie künftig als Orte der Begegnung nutzen zu

CO_2 emissions by 90%. In the summer of 2012 the renovation work in the first houses of the neighbourhood in the north-western part of Frankfurt was completed: The facades have been insulated, the windows replaced and enlarged, the bathrooms renovated, balconies built and entrances were designed to be more friendly so that in the future they and the neighbourhood courtyards might become social areas. On the western edge is the centrally connecting Ludwig-Landmann-Straße, a new focus and a proper Entrée. This was very important for the inhabitants of the settlement who also lobbied for a new supermarket. The project can serve as a model for other districts and cities.

As Heinrich-Lübke-Straße bends to the right we go up the steps next to the new building.

Heinrich-Lübke-Siedlung:

Model for the re-development of a large urban district

Heinrich-Lübke-Siedlung:

Energetic level
| Existing buildings: undercut the *EnEV* 2009 for renovations by about 55%
| New residential buildings: *Passive Houses*
| Commercial Space: according to *EnEV*

Nutzung (erneuerbarer) Energien
| Connection to the *district heating* network with its own heating system
| Roof areas: solar panels, *photovoltaic*
| Natural lighting and ventilation
| Ventilation system with *heat recovery*

Characteristic, tip
During the current renovation/modernization the tenants remain in their homes and are, where possible, involved in the transformation. This participatory approach led to the first nomination in 2011 for the city of Frankfurt for the 'Eurocities Award'. The prize is awarded to cities that want to improve the quality of life of its residents.

Heinrich-Lübke-Siedlung/Settlement

Heinrich-Lübke-Siedlung:

Besonderheit, Tipp
Während der laufenden Sanierung/Modernisierung verbleiben die Mieter in ihren Wohnungen und werden, soweit möglich, in die Umgestaltung mit einbezogen. Dieses Beteiligungskonzept führte 2011 zur erstmaligen Nominierung der Stadt Frankfurt für den ‚Eurocities Award'. Der Preis wird an Städte verliehen, die die Lebensqualität ihrer Einwohner stark verbessern möchten.

Riedberg:

Nachhaltiger, neuer Stadtteil mit Konzept der kurzen Wege

Riedberg:

Auftraggeber/ Contractor
Stadt Frankfurt am Main

Entwicklungsträger, Projektbetreuung/ Project development and support
HA Hessen Agentur GmbH, HA Stadtentwicklungsgesellschaft mbH

Architekt/Architect
Anerkannte Architekten und Stadtplaner/Well-known architects and urban planners

Heinrich-Lübke-Siedlung/Settlement

können – ebenso wie die individuellen ‚Nachbarschaftshöfe'. Die Siedlung erhielt an ihrem westlichen Rand, der zentrale Verbindungen schaffenden Ludwig-Landmann-Straße, einen neuen Mittelpunkt und ein richtiges Entrée. Darauf hatten die Bewohner großen Wert gelegt. Sie nutzten die Möglichkeit der Mitsprache auch, um für einen neuen Supermarkt eindringlich zu werben. Das Projekt kann als Vorbild für andere Stadtteile und Städte dienen. An der Rechtsbiegung der Heinrich-Lübke-Straße laufen wir die Treppe geradeaus neben dem Neubau hinauf. Dann halten wir uns links, an der Ludwig-Landmann-Straße rechts. Auf der linken Seite sehen wir den Beginn der Ernst-May-Siedlung Praunheim und die U-Bahnstation ‚Praunheim Heerstraße'.

... mit der U8, U9 oder dem Bus 29

Die Haltestelle ‚Uni Campus Riedberg' liegt mitten in unserem Zielgebiet. Wenn wir das Zentrum mit der Frankfurter Sparkasse links von uns lassen und der Altenhöferallee nordwärts folgen, erreichen wir links das **Gymnasium Riedberg**, unmittelbar am Kätcheslachpark. Der Bau hat Ende 2010 begonnen und soll 2013 fertig gestellt sein. Das *Passivhaus*-Projekt für 1.350 Schüler umfasst neben dem Schulbau ein Jugendhaus

Then we bear left at the Ludwig-Landmann-Straße on the right. On the left we see the beginning of Ernst-May-Siedlung in Praunheim and the underground station 'Praunheim Heerstraße'.

... with the U8, U9 or the bus 29

The station 'Uni Campus Riedberg' is in the middle of our area of interest. If we leave the centre with the Frankfurter Sparkasse to the left and follow Altenhöferallee northbound, we reach the **Riedberg Grammar School** on the left directly at Kätcheslach Park. The construction began in late 2010 and is due for completion in 2013. The *Passive House* project for 1,350 students includes the school building a youth centre and a sports hall with three fields. The structure assigns each different functional area its own clearly perceivable form.

The possibility of residing, living, learning and research together in one place – this is where the main emphasis lies for the 'green' **district of Riedberg** in the northwest of the Main metropolis. In one of the largest urban development projects in Germany approximately 6,000 residential units for 15,000 residents will be developed and 3,000 jobs in services, science and research will be created. The well-developed

Riedberg:

Sustainable, new district with concept of short distances

Riedberg:

Energetic level
| Residential and commercial buildings: At least 30% below current *EnEV* and *Passive Houses*
| Schools, day care centres: *Passive Houses*

Use (renewable) energy
| Supply of *district heating* generated in energy-efficient *combined heat and power* plants
| Energy-efficient building technology
| Rainwater management
| Green spaces, natural ventilation and lighting

Riedberg, Zentrum/Centre

6 | Exkursionen

Riedberg:

Entwicklungsdauer/
Development time
1997–2017

Gesamtfläche/
Total area
267 ha

Energetisches Niveau
| Wohn- und Gewerbebauten: Mindestens 30% unter jeweils aktueller *EnEV* und *Passivhäuser*
| Schulen, Kindertagesstätten: *Passivhäuser*

Nutzung (erneuerbarer) Energien
| Versorgung mit *Fernwärme*, in energieeffizienter *Kraft-Wärme-Kopplung* erzeugt
| Energieeffiziente Gebäudetechnik
| Regenwasserbewirtschaftung
| Grünflächen, natürliche Lüftung und Belichtung

Besonderheit, Tipp
Der Stadtteil, seine Quartiere sowie einzelne seiner Bauten können im Rahmen von Führungen besichtigt werden. Nähere Informationen dazu bei:
Infobüro Riedberg
Tel.: 069-95 11 66 0
E-Mail: riedberg@ha-stadtentwicklung.de
www.riedberg.de

Architektur im Dialog
www.architekturimdialog.de

und eine Drei-Feld-Sporthalle. Der gegliederte Baukörper weist den einzelnen Funktionsbereichen jeweils eigene, klar ablesbare Volumina zu. Wohnen, Leben, Lernen, Forschen – unter diesen Leitthemen entsteht der grüne **Stadtteil Riedberg** im Nordwesten der Mainmetropole. In einem der größten städtebaulichen Vorhaben Deutschlands werden etwa 6.000 Wohneinheiten für 15.000 Einwohner und für Dienstleistung, Wissenschaft und Forschung etwa 3.000 Arbeitsplätze geschaffen. Das gut erschlossene Riedberg-Gebiet setzt sich aus sieben einzelnen Quartieren zusammen, eines davon bildet der naturwissenschaftliche Campus der Goethe-Universität mit etwa 8.000 Studierenden. Der eigenständige Stadtteil bezieht seinen Charme aus seiner besonderen topographischen Lage, seinem städtebaulichen Gesamtkonzept und der qualitätvollen Architektur. Im Gegensatz zu Trabantenstädten und Großsiedlungen vergangener Jahre wird die neue Riedbergbebauung durch städtische Strukturen und Raumfolgen geprägt sein. Die Mischung unterschiedlichster Bevölkerungsgruppen und Nutzungen sorgt für Lebendigkeit. Alles ist fußläufig erreichbar. Über ein Drittel des gesamten Areals sind öffentliche Freiflächen. Ein Rundweg bindet den Stadtteil an Frankfurts Grüngürtel an. Die öffentlichen Einrichtungen, Eigentums- und Mietwohnungen, Senioren- und Studentenwohnungen werden in unterschiedlichen Formen des energieeffizienten Bauens realisiert – inklusive *Passivhaus*standard und als Plus-Energie-Haus. Gleichzeitig entwickelt sich mit der ‚Science City' ein hochkarätiger Wissenschafts- und Technologiestandort.

Wir folgen der Altenhöferallee mit Blick auf die Skyline bergab und biegen hinter der Bus-Haltestelle ‚Geozentrum' links in einen schmalen Weg ein. Wo er auf einen Spielplatz trifft, blei-

Riedberg

Riedberg district consists of seven individual areas; one of them is the scientific campus of the Goethe University, with about 8,000 students. The independent district's charm is its special topography, its urban concept and the quality architecture. Unlike satellite towns and large settlements of the past, the new Riedberg development will be characterized by urban structures and space. The mixture of different population groups and uses ensures vitality. Everything is within walking distance. More than a third of the whole area is dedicated to public open spaces. A circular route links the district to Frankfurt's green belt. The public facilities, condominiums and rental apartments, senior and student housing will be built in various forms of energy-efficient construction – including *Passive House* standard and Plus Energy House types. At the same time a top-class location for science and technology is under development in the 'Science City'.

We follow the Altenhöferallee downhill, overlooking the Frankfurt skyline, and behind the bus station 'Geozentrum' turn left into a narrow path. The path leads us to a playground where we keep right and follow the **Bonifatiuspark** and stroll along the natural stone wall.

Riedberg:

Characteristic, tip
The district, its neighbourhoods as well as its individual buildings can be visited on guided tours. For more information, contact:

Infobüro Riedberg
Phone: 069 - 95 11 66 0
E-Mail: riedberg@ha-stadtentwicklung.de
www.riedberg.de

Architektur im Dialog
www.architekturimdialog.de

Oberhalb der Natursteinmauer an der Straße ‚Zur Kalbacher Höhe' ist die letzte von 10 Stationen des etwa 7,5 km langen Geopfads ‚Stadt-Land-Fluss'. Informationstafeln zeigen, was sich alles unter dem Begriff ‚Geo' verbirgt. An den meisten Stationen gibt es auch spezielle Angebote für Kinder. Nähere Informationen unter: www.geopfad-frankfurt.de

Grundschule Riedberg/Primary School

ben wir rechts und befinden uns im **Bonifatiuspark**, den wir an einer Natursteinmauer entlang schlendern.

An der Straße ‚Zur Kalbacher Höhe' gehen wir nach links und erreichen bei Nr. 15 eine Grundschule mit Kita und Turnhalle. In dem hoch wärmegedämmten Massivbau können seit Ende 2004 bis zu 400 Kinder unterrichtet werden. Die **Grundschule Riedberg** war die 1. Frankfurter Schule im *Passivhaus*standard und die 2. ihrer Art in Deutschland. Ihre energiesparende und umweltschonende Bauweise reduziert den Primärenergiebedarf auf 59 kWh/(m^{2}a). Die Schule spart jährlich über 50.000 € Energiekosten. Die *Photovoltaik*anlage und Holzpelletheizung vermeiden zusammen jährlich rund 71 t CO_2.

Wir folgen der Straße bergauf und kommen so zur U-Bahnstation ‚Riedberg'.

Bonifatiuspark

> Above the stone wall along the road Zur Kalbacher Höhe is the last of 10 stations of the 7.5km long Geo-Trail, 'Stadt-Land-Fluss' (City-Country-River). Information boards explain what is meant by the term, 'Geo'. At most stations, there are also special activities for children. For more information: www.geopfad-frankfurt.de

At 'Zur Kalbacher Höhe' we go to the left and reach a primary school with a nursery and gymnasium at No. 15. Since the end of 2004 up to 400 children are able to be educated in this highly insulated solid building. This **primary school in Riedberg** was the first school in Frankfurt and the second of its kind in Germany to be built to *Passive House* standards. Its energy-saving and environmentally friendly design reduces the primary energy demand to 59 kWh/(m²a). The school saves over € 50,000 annually in energy costs. The *photovoltaic* system and wood pellet heating system avoid around 71 tons of CO_2 a year.

We follow the road uphill and arrive at the subway station 'Riedberg'.

Service

Adressen/
Address information

Informationen, Projekte, Veranstaltungen rund um Frankfurt als Green City/Informations, projects, events about Frankfurt as green city: www.frankfurt-greencity.de

Frankfurter Agenda-Stadtplan für nachhaltiges Wirtschaften und Genießen/Map for sustainable economic activities and enjoyment: www.umweltforum-rhein-main.de

Auskunft/Information

Tourismus+Congress GmbH Frankfurt am Main
Kaiserstraße 56
T.: 069-21 23 88 00
www.frankfurt-tourismus.de

Tourist Information Hauptbahnhof, Empfangshalle/ Central railway station, entrance hall
Mo–Fr 8.00–21.00 Uhr,
Sa–So + Feiertage/Holidays
9.00–18.00 Uhr

Tourist Information Römer
Römerberg 27
Mo–Fr 9.30–17.30 Uhr,
Sa–So + Feiertage/Holidays
9.30–16.00 Uhr

Verkehrsmittel/
Transportation

nextbike –
24h Fahrradverleihsystem
T. Service + Verleih/Rental:
030-69 20 50 46
www.nextbike.de
Saison je nach Witterung: etwa März bis November/ Weather-dependent: march to november

Stadtwerke Verkehrsgesellschaft Frankfurt am Main mbH VGF-Kundenzentrum
Kurt-Schumacher-Straße 8
T.: 069-19 449
www.vgf-ffm.de
Mo–Fr 8.00–17.00 Uhr

Velotaxi Frankfurt M. Graf
Leopold-Wertheimer Str. 8
61130 Nidderau
T.: 069-71 58 88 55
Velo: 0700 83 56 82 94
www.frankfurt.velotaxi.de
Täglich/Daily 12.00–20.00 Uhr, von November bis März nur auf Reservierung/ November to march: reservation requiered

In den Routen genannte Museen/Museums mentioned in tours

Archäologisches Museum Frankfurt
Karmelitergasse 1
T.: 069-21 23 58 96
www.archaeologisches-museum.frankfurt.de
Di–So 10.00–18.00 Uhr,
Mi 10.00–20.00 Uhr

Deutsches Architekturmuseum
Schaumainkai 43
T.: 069-21 23 88 44
www.dam-online.de
Di+Do–Sa 11.00–18.00 Uhr,
So 11.00–19.00 Uhr,
Mi 11.00–20.00 Uhr

Deutsches Filmmuseum und Deutsches Filminstitut
Schaumainkai 41
T.: 069-96 12 20 220
www.deutsches-filminstitut.de/filmmuseum
Di+Do–So 10.00–18.00 Uhr,
Mi 10.00–20.00 Uhr

Dommuseum
Domplatz 14
T.: 069-13 37 61 86
www.dommuseum-frankfurt.de
Di–Fr 10.00–17.00 Uhr,
Sa–So + Feiertage/Holidays
11.00–17.00 Uhr

Frankfurter Goethe-Museum und Goethe-Haus
Großer Hirschgraben 23–25
T.: 069-13 88 00
www.goethehaus-frankfurt.de
Mo–Sa 10.00–18.00 Uhr,
So + Feiertage/Holidays
10.00–17.30 Uhr

Frankfurter Kunstverein
Steinernes Haus am Römerberg, Markt 44
T.: 069-21 93 140
www.fkv.de
Di + Do + Fr 11.00–19.00 Uhr, Mi 11.00–21.00 Uhr,
Sa + So 10.00–19.00 Uhr

Historisches Museum Frankfurt
Fahrtor 2 (Römerberg)
T.: 069-21 23 51 54
www.historisches-museum.frankfurt.de
Di–So 10.00–18.00 Uhr,
Mi 10.00–21.00 Uhr

Ikonen-Museum der Stadt Frankfurt – Stiftung Dr. Schmidt-Voigt
Brückenstraße 3–7
T.: 069-21 23 62 62
www.ikonenmuseum-frankfurt.de
Di–So 10.00–17.00 Uhr,
Mi 10.00–20.00 Uhr

Institut für Stadtgeschichte, Karmeliterkloster
Münzgasse 9
T.: 069-21 23 84 25
www.stadtgeschichte-ffm.de
Institut und Lesesaal/ Institute and reading room:
Mo–Fr 8.30–17.00 Uhr
Ausstellungen/Exhibitions:
Mo–Fr 10.00–18.00 Uhr,
Sa + So 11.00–18.00 Uhr

Service

Jüdisches Museum
der Stadt Frankfurt am Main
Untermainkai 14/15
T.: 069-21 23 50 00
www.juedischesmuseum.de
Di–So 10.00–17.00 Uhr,
Mi 10.00–20.00 Uhr

Liebieghaus Skulpturensammlung,
Städtische Galerie
Schaumainkai 71
T.: 069-65 00 490
www.liebieghaus.de
Di + Fr–So 10.00–18.00 Uhr,
Mi + Do 10.00–21.00 Uhr

Museum Angewandte Kunst
Frankfurt
Schaumainkai 17
T.: 069-21 23 40 37
www.angewandtekunst-frankfurt.de
Di + Do–So 10.00–17.00 Uhr,
Mi 10.00–21.00 Uhr

Museum für Komische
Kunst, Caricatura Museum
Frankfurt
Weckmarkt 17
T.: 069-21 23 01 61
www.caricatura-museum.de
Di–So 10.00–18.00 Uhr,
Mi 10.00–21.00 Uhr

Museum für Kommunikation
Frankfurt
Schaumainkai 53
T.: 069-60 600
www.mfk-frankfurt.de
Di–Fr 9.00–18.00 Uhr,
Sa–So + Feiertage/Holidays
11.00–19.00 Uhr

MMK
Museum für Moderne Kunst
Domstraße 10
T.: 069-21 23 04 47
www.mmk-frankfurt.de
Di + Do–So 10.00–18.00 Uhr,
Mi 10.00–20.00 Uhr

Museum Giersch
Schaumainkai 83
T.: 069-63 30 41 28
www.museum-giersch.de
Di–Do 12.00–19.00 Uhr,
Fr–So 10.00–18.00 Uhr

Portikus
Alte Brücke 2 (Maininsel)
T.: 069-96 24 45 40
www.portikus.de
Di–So 11.00–18.00 Uhr,
Mi 11.00–20.00 Uhr

Schirn Kunsthalle
Frankfurt am Main GmbH
Römerberg
T.: 069-29 98 820
www.schirn.de
Di + Fr–So 10.00–19.00 Uhr,
Mi + Do 10.00–22.00 Uhr

Senckenberg Forschungsinstitut und Naturmuseum
Senckenberganlage 25
T.: 069-75 420
www.senckenberg.de/
frankfurt
Mo–Di + Do–Fr 9.00–17.00
Uhr, Mi 9.00–20.00 Uhr,
Sa–So + Feiertage/Holidays
9.00–18.00 Uhr

Städel Museum
Schaumainkai 63
T.: 069-60 50 980
www.staedelmuseum.de
Di + Fr–So 10.00–18.00 Uhr,
Mi + Do 10.00–21.00 Uhr

Weltkulturen Museum
Schaumainkai 29–37
T.: 069-21 23 59 13
www.weltkulturenmuseum.de
Di + Do–So 11.00–18.00 Uhr,
Mi 11.00–20.00 Uhr

Tipps/Tips

Frankfurt Card
Ticket: 1 Tag/Day 9,20 €
2 Tage/Days 13,50 €

Gruppenkarte (für max. 5
Personen)/Group card for up
to 5 people: 1 Tag/Day 19,00
€, 2 Tage/Days 28,00 €

Öffentlicher Nahverkehr
im Stadtgebiet Frankfurt,
einschließlich des Flughafens, und Ermäßigungen für
zahlreiche Einrichtungen.
Erhältlich an den Tourist Informationen, am Flughafen
Frankfurt Main, an der Verkehrsinsel an der Hauptwache, bei allen Ticketcornern
und in ausgewählten Hotels.
Public transport in the city
of Frankfurt and its airport,
rebates at numerous places.
Available at: Tourist Informations, Frankfurt airport,
Hauptwache, ticket shops
and selected hotels.

MuseumsuferTicket
2 Tage hintereinander 34
Museen besuchen/Visit 34
museums at 2 consecutive
days:
Regulär/Regular 18 €
Familie/Family 28 €
ermäßigt/reduced 10 €

Besichtigung des 1. Frankfurter Windgenerators,
Inbetriebnahme 2008, mit
der Sonderführung ‚Erneuerbare Energie'/Visit Frankfurt's 1st wind generator at:

Explora – Science Center
Frankfurt
Glauburgplatz 1
T.: 069-78 88 88
www.exploramuseum.de
Mo–So 11.00–18.00 Uhr

Objekte im öffentlichen
Raum/Informations about
art in public places:
www.kunst-im-oeffentlichen-raum-frankfurt.de

Kalender/Calendar

Januar/January

- Messen/Trade fairs: Christmasworld, Creativeworld, Paperworld

Februar/February

- Deutscher Opernball
- Großer Frankfurter Fastnachtszug
- Messe/Trade fair: Facility Management

März/March

- Messe ISH oder Light+Building (im Wechsel)/ Trade fair ISH or Light+Building (in turn)
- Luminale (parallel zur Light+Building, alle geraden Jahre)/ Luminale (during Light+Building, every straight year)
- Frühjahrs-Dippemess
- Apfelwein im Römer

April/April

- Lange Nacht der Museen
- Musikmesse

Mai/May

- Eschborn-Frankfurt City Loop
- Goetheturmfest
- Wäldchestag
- Grüne-Soße-Festival
- Wolkenkratzer-Festival (unregelmäßig/sporadic)

Marktstand/Market stand

Shopping

Beim Energiereferat der Stadt Frankfurt am Main ist unter anderem die Broschüre ‚Klimagourmet – Genießen und das Klima schützen' kostenfrei erhältlich. Darüber hinaus kann dort die Wanderausstellung ‚Green it – weltverträglich kommunizieren' ausgeliehen werden. Sie betrachtet den Lebenszyklus von elektronischen Geräten. Nähere Informationen unter: www.energiereferat.stadt-frankfurt.de

Märkte – Regional, saisonal, einzigartig

Mo – Sa: An 60 Ständen in der Frankfurter Kleinmarkthalle (Hasengasse 5–7) finden Sie außergewöhnliche und hochwertige Produkte, die es sonst kaum zu kaufen gibt. Ein besonderer Tipp ist die Weinterrasse im Obergeschoss.
Di + Do: Kaisermarkt am Hauptbahnhof
Mi + Sa: Bornheimer Wochenmarkt auf der Berger Straße
Do: Bockenheimer Wochenmarkt an der Bockenheimer Warte
Do + Sa: Bauern- und Erzeugermarkt auf der Konstablerwache
Fr: Schillermarkt in der Schillerstraße nördlich der Hauptwache
Sa: Am Schaumainkai zwischen dem Eisernen Steg und dem Holbeinsteg sowie am Osthafenplatz entlang der Lindleystraße findet jeweils wöchentlich wechselnd von 9.00–14.00 Uhr der Frankfurter Flohmarkt statt.

Fairtrade

Frankfurt am Main hat am 24. Januar 2011 die Auszeichnung ‚Fairtrade Stadt' erhalten. Folgende Plattform zeigt die Organisationen, die sich hier für den fairen Handel stark machen, und Geschäfte, in denen Sie Fairtrade-Waren erstehen oder konsumieren können: www.fairtradetown-frankfurt.de

Reparaturservice ‚Frankfurt repariert selbst'

Die Frankfurter Entsorgungs- und Service GmbH gibt online eine Übersicht zu Frankfurter Betrieben, die Reparaturen anbieten – vom Fahrrad bis zur Telekommunikation. Darüber hinaus bekommen Sie Hinweise für den Ersatzteilverkauf und zu Second-Hand-Waren:
www.tinyurl.com/auzy9f8

Shopping

At the Energy Department of the City of Frankfurt, amongst others, the brochure, 'Climate Gourmet – Enjoy and protect the environment' is available free of charge. In addition, you can also borrow the portable exhibition, 'Green it – communicate environmentally friendly'. It considers the life cycle of electronic devices. For more information: www.energiereferat. stadt-frankfurt.de

Markets – Regional, seasonal, unique

Mon – Sat: At 60 stalls in Frankfurt's Kleinmarkthalle (Hasengasse 5–7, Small Market Hall) you can find unusual and high quality products, which are otherwise difficult to obtain. A special tip is the wine terrace on the upper floor.
Tue + Thu: Kaisermarkt at the main Railway Station
Wed + Sat: Bornheimer Weekly Market on Berger Straße
Thu: Bockenheimer Erzeugermarkt Weekly Produce Market on Bockenheimer Warte
Thu + Sat: Farmers & Producers Market on Konstablerwache
Fri: Schiller market in Schillerstraße north of the Hauptwache
Sat: Either at Schaumainkai between the Eisernen Steg and the Holbeinsteg or at Osthafenplatz (eastern Harbour place) along Lindleystraße there is an weekly alternating flea market which takes place from 9.00 am – 2.00 pm.

Fair trade

Frankfurt am Main was designated with the award, 'Fairtrade City' on 24th January 2011. The following websites show the organisations which follow the principle of fair trade and shops in which fair trade products can be bought or consumed www.fairtradetown-frankfurt.de

Repair service 'Frankfurt DIY Repairs'

The Frankfurt disposal and Service GmbH provides an online overview of Frankfurt companies which offer repairs – from bicycles to telecommunications. In addition, you get tips for the sale of spare parts and second-hand goods: www.tinyurl.com/auzy9f8

Frankfurt's Honey

The artist duo, 'Finger', have been beekeepers since 2007 in the City and produce here Frankfurt's city honey. After the first beehive installation at the social service station in Bahnhofsviertel others quickly followed; for example on the roof of the Museum of Modern Art (MMK). In another project, 'Frankfurt summt' (Frankfurt buzzes), companies participate like the KfW banking group or the Jumeirah Hotels, Westin Grand and Goldman 25Hours. The honey is available in the Senckenberg Natural History Museum shop and the MMK shop, where you can also see the bees.

Service

Kalender/Calendar

Juni/June

- Fressgass'-Fest
- Tag der Architektur
- Rosen- und Lichterfest im Palmengarten
- Opernplatzfest
- Höchster Schlossfest

Juli/July

- Frankfurter CSD
- Opel Ironman Germany Triathlon

August/August

- Mainfest
- Museumsuferfest
- Sachsenhäuser Brunnenfest
- Apfelweinfestival

September/September

- Rheingauer Weinmarkt
- Herbst-Dippemess
- Messe/Trade fair domicil
- Internationale Automobil-Ausstellung (IAA, alle ungeraden Jahre/ every odd year)

Oktober/October

- BMW Frankfurt Marathon
- Buchmesse/Book Fair
- Deutsches Jazzfestival Frankfurt

November/November

- Deutscher Sportpresseball

Dezember/December

- Weihnachtsmarkt/ Christmas market

Frankfurter Honig

Das Künstlerduo ‚finger' imkert seit 2007 in der City und erzeugt hier Frankfurter Stadthonig. Nach der Diakonie im Bahnhofsviertel folgten schnell weitere Installationen, zum Beispiel auf dem Dach des Museums für Moderne Kunst (MMK). Bei einem anderen Projekt, ‚Frankfurt summt', beteiligen sich Unternehmen wie die KfW-Bankengruppe oder die Hotels Jumeirah, Westin Grand und Goldman 25Hours. Erhältlich ist der Honig im Shop des Senckenberg Naturmuseums und des MMK, wo Sie die Bienen auch jeweils beobachten können.

Unterwegs in der Stadt mit 52% grünen Freiräumen und Wasserflächen

Parks und Gärten

Zu den Juwelen gehören der Bethmannpark mit seiner vielfältigen Blütenpracht in der Stadtmitte, der Adolph-von-Holzhausen-Park mit einem Wasserschlösschen im Nordend, der weitläufige Grüneburgpark im Westend und der Günthersburgpark in Bornheim mit ihrem alten Baumbestand und ihren großen Wiesenflächen sowie der barocke Bolongarogarten in Höchst. Zudem sind der Volkspark Niddatal im Nordwesten, der Rebstockpark hinter der Messe, der Ostpark und der Park auf dem 180 m hohen Lohrberg beliebte Ausflugsziele. Bedeutender Teil der Grünflächen ist auch der 80 ha große Hauptfriedhof.

Mainufer

Am nördlichen Mainufer zeigt sich Frankfurt von seiner mediterranen Seite. Zwischen Untermain- und Friedensbrücke liegen die Nizza-Gärten, in denen Feigen, Bitterorangen, Zitronen, Palmen, Zedern und ein Ginkgobaum gedeihen.

Wallanlagen

Die Parkanlage Anlagenring erstreckt sich auf einem rund 5 km langen Halbkreis um die Innenstadt und folgt dem Verlauf der mittelalterlichen Stadtmauern. Die Spazierwege sind von Brunnen, Teichen, Skulpturen, Denk- und Mahnmalen gesäumt.

Frankfurter Grüngürtel

Durch den Grüngürtel führen ein 64,5 km langer Rundwanderweg und ein 63 km langer Radrundweg. Tipps zu dem Naherholungsgebiet im Frankfurter Stadtgebiet mit seinen verschiedenen Freizeitangeboten, Naturschutzgebieten und Rastplätzen finden Sie unter:
www.tinyurl.com/cec9v5a

Stadtwald

Im Süden des Grüngürtels liegt Deutschlands größter Stadtwald. Die über 5.000 ha Bewaldung durchzieht ein 450 km langes Wegenetz. Spaziergänger, Jogger, Radfahrer und Reiter können so viele Sehenswürdigkeiten und auch die nördlich des Mains liegenden kleine (Auen)Wälder erleben:
www.tinyurl.com/cy5r7sd

Radwege

Tipps und Informationen rund um Radwege, -routen und -service in Frankfurt:
www.radfahren-ffm.de

Der Main-Radweg gehört zu den schönsten Radfernwegen Deutschlands. Als erste Route in Deutschland trägt er das Gütesiegel ‚Qualitätsradroute mit fünf Sternen' des ADFC:
www.mainradweg.com

Around and about the city with 52% green areas and water surfaces

Parks & Gardens

The finest of Frankfurt's park areas are Bethmann Park with its varied flowerage in the city centre, the Adolph-von-Holzhausen-Park with a small moated castle in Nordend, the sprawling Grüneburg Park in the Westend and Günthersburg Park in Bornheim with its old tree population and its large meadows as well as the Baroque Bolongarogarten in Höchst. In addition, the Volkspark Niddatal in the northwest, the Rebstock Park behind the exhibition centre, the Ostpark and the park on the 180m high Lohrberg are popular destinations. The 80 hectare main cemetery also has a significant proportion of green area.

River Main Embankment

On the northern bank of the Main, Frankfurt has a Mediterranean flair. Between Untermain Bridge and the Friedensbrücke are the Nice Gardens in which figs, bitter oranges, lemons, palm trees, cedars, and a ginkgo tree flourish.

City Walls

The park, Anlagenring, stretches along a 5km long, semi-circular, green belt around the city and follows the course of the medieval city walls. The walkways are lined with fountains, ponds, sculptures, monuments and memorials.

Frankfurt's Green Belt

A 64.5 km walking trail and a 63 km long cycle route lead you through the Green Belt. For recreation tips in the Frankfurt area, with its variety of outdoor activities, nature reserves and recreation areas, visit:
www.tinyurl.com/cec9v5a

Urban Forest

In the south of the green belt is Germany's largest city forest. The 5,000 hectare forest has a network of paths totalling 450km. Walkers, joggers, cyclists and horse riders can see a variety of attractions here as well as in the small woods (floodplains) north of the river:
www.tinyurl.com/cy5r7sd

Cycle Paths

For tips and information about cycling routes and its services in Frankfurt, go to:
www.radfahren-ffm.de

The Main-Radweg (river cycle path) is one of the finest long-distance routes in Germany. It is the first route in Germany to carry the seal of 'Premium route with five stars' from the ADFC:
www.mainradweg.com

Glossar

Adiabate Kühlung
Gebäudekühlung ohne zusätzlichen Energiebedarf. Dabei wird insbesondere Verdunstungskälte von Wasser in einem abgeschlossenen Innenraum genutzt, um die Raumluft abzukühlen.

Bauteilaktivierung
Eine thermische Bauteilaktivierung, auch Betonkernaktivierung genannt, nutzt die Massen eines Gebäudes zur alleinigen oder ergänzenden Regulierung der Raumtemperatur. Der Begriff stammt aus der Klimatechnik.

Blockheizkraftwerk (BHKW)
Ein BHKW ist eine modular aufgebaute Anlage zur Erzeugung von elektrischem Strom und Wärme. Unter Einsatz des Prinzips der Kraft-Wärme-Kopplung speist die Anlage Nutzwärme in ein Fernwärmenetz ein oder nutzt die Abwärme aus der Stromerzeugung direkt am Ort des Wärmeverbrauchs. Dies führt zu einem gegenüber der gängigen Kombination von lokaler Heizung und zentralem Großkraftwerk erhöhten Gesamtwirkungsgrad.

DGNB, Deutsche Gesellschaft für Nachhaltiges Bauen e. V.
2007 von 16 Initiatoren unterschiedlicher Fachrichtungen der Bau- und Immobilienbranche gegründet, will sie die Planung, den Bau und Betrieb von nachhaltigen Gebäuden voranbringen. Im Fokus steht das seit 2008 existierende Zertifizierungssystem. Es bewertet den Lebenszyklus eines Bauwerks, seine ökologischen, ökonomischen, soziokulturellen, funktionalen und technischen Aspekte, ebenso die Prozess- und Standortqualität. Abhängig von dem Nutzungsprofil (Bauwerkstyp im Neubau oder Bestand) und den dafür definierten Kriterien wird eine Auszeichnung in Bronze (Gesamterfüllungsgrad ab 50%), Silber (ab 65%) oder Gold (ab 80%) vergeben.

Energieeinsparverordnung (EnEV) 2002, 2004, 2007, 2009
Die Verordnung über energiesparenden Wärmeschutz und energiesparende Anlagentechnik bei Gebäuden ist Teil des deutschen Wirtschaftsverwaltungsrechts. Sie definiert die für Neubauten und Sanierungen verbindlichen energetischen Standards, insbesondere den Jahresprimärenergiebedarf. Mit der EnEV wurden die Heizungsanlagenverordnung und die Wärmeschutzverordnung abgelöst und zusammen geführt. Die nächste Novellierung soll in 2013 erfolgen.

Erneuerbare Energien
Auch als regenerative oder alternative Energien bezeichnet, sind Energieträger aus Quellen, die sich nach dem menschlichen Ermessen relativ schnell erneuern können oder unerschöpflich sind. Zu ihnen gehören die solare Strahlung, Erdwärme, Wind- und Wasserkräfte sowie die Biomasse/nachwachsende Rohstoffe.

Fernwärme
Wärmelieferung für die Gebäudeheizung und die Bereitstellung von Warmwasser. Die benötigte Wärme wird bei der Stromerzeugung in zentralen Heizkraftwerken gewonnen. Ihr Transport erfolgt über ein wärmegedämmtes, meist erdverlegtes Rohrsystem, das einzelne Gebäude, Stadtteile oder Städte versorgen kann.

Graue Energie
Sie bezeichnet die gesamte Energiemenge, die zur Her- und Bereitstellung sowie zur Entsorgung eines Produkts oder einer Dienstleistung direkt und indirekt aufgewendet werden muss. Sie differenziert dabei zwischen erneuerbarer und fossiler Energie und bezieht sich auf einen spezifischen Produktions- und Bereitstellungsort.

Grauwasser
Wenig verschmutztes Abwasser, wie es zum Beispiel beim Händewaschen oder Duschen anfällt. Es kann zu Brauch- oder Betriebswasser aufbereitet und so für Toilettenspülungen oder die Kühlung von Maschinen weiter genutzt werden. Der Einsatz von Grau- oder Regenwasser ist umweltfreundlich, da die entsprechend benötigte Menge nicht durch aufwendig aufbereitetes Frischwasser gedeckt werden muss.

Green Building Frankfurt/ FrankfurtRheinMain
Als ‚Green Building Frankfurt' (2009) oder ‚Green Building FrankfurtRheinMain' (2011) werden Gebäude ausgezeichnet, die innovativ, gestalterisch hochwertig und nachhaltig sind und somit Vorbildfunktion für andere Projekte haben. Der Preis wird seit 2009 alle zwei Jahre vergeben, aktuell von den Städten Frankfurt am Main, Darmstadt und dem Regionalverband FrankfurtRheinMain.

Glossary

Adiabatic cooling
Cooling a building without additional energy requirements; especially through the use of the cooling effects of evaporating water in a closed space.

Brine
Salt-water solution, which is used as a heat transfer medium for geothermal energy, e.g. in heat pumps and geothermal probes.

Combined heat and power (CHP)
CHP is the simultaneous conversion of an energy source into electricity and useable heat in a stationary technical installation.

Combined heat and power unit (CHP)
A CHP is a modular system for the production of electricity and heat. Using the principle of combined heat and power, the system produces heat into a distribution network or uses the waste heat from power generation locally. This increases the overall efficiency compared to the conventional combination of local heating and central power plant.

Component activation
Thermal component activation, also known as concrete core activation, uses the mass of a building for the exclusive or additional controlling of room temperatures. The term arises from the air conditioning technology.

DGNB, German Association for Sustainable Building
Founded in 2007 by the initiators of 16 different fields of the construction and real estate industry, it wants to promote the planning, constructing and operating of sustainable buildings. The existing certification system has operated since 2008. It evaluates the life cycle of a building, its ecological, economic, socio-cultural, functional and technical aspects as well as the process and location quality. Depending on the usage profile (structure type new or existing) and on the defined criteria bronze (total performance level exceeding 50%), silver (over 65%) or gold (80% and above) awards are assigned.

District heating
Heat supply for building heating and provision of hot water. The heat required is recovered during electricity production in central heating plants. It is transported via a thermally insulated, usually buried, piping system that can heat individual buildings, neighbourhoods or cities.

Ecological balance
This is defined in DIN EN ISO 14040 and DIN EN ISO 14044. Based on the used materials it calculates the production process of a product in its environmental impact and its influence (e.g. emissions). The methodology is also applicable for the investigation of processes, procedures and businesses.

Energy saving guidelines (EnEV) 2002, 2004, 2007, 2009
The regulations on energy-saving heat insulation and energy-saving system engineering for buildings are part of the German economic administrative law. It defines the mandatory energy standards for new buildings and renovations, especially the annual primary energy requirement. The EnEV replaced the heating system and insulation regulations by combining them. The next amendment is due to take place in 2013.

Green Building Frankfurt/FrankfurtRheinMain
Buildings that are innovative, sustainable and have a high design-quality and thus are models for other projects are awarded as 'Green Building Frankfurt' (2009) or 'Green Building FrankfurtRheinMain' (2011). The prize has been presented every two years since 2009, currently by the cities of Frankfurt, Darmstadt and the Regional Association FrankfurtRheinMain.

Grey (embodied) energy
It denotes the total amount of energy that is needed directly and indirectly for the production, deployment and disposal of a product or service. It differentiates between renewable and fossil energy and is related to a specific production and deployment location.

Grey water (sullage)
Slightly dirty wastewater, as obtained, for example, from hand washing or showering. It can be processed into domestic or industrial water and thus be reused for flushing toilets or cooling equipment. The use of grey water or rainwater is environmentally friendly, since the required amount does not have to be covered by processed fresh water.

Glossar

Kraft-Wärme-Kopplung (KWK)
KWK ist die gleichzeitige Umwandlung eines Energieträgers in elektrische Energie und Nutzwärme in einer ortsfesten technischen Anlage.

Lebenszyklusanalyse
Die Lebenszyklusanalyse (Life Cycle Assessment – LCA) bilanziert den Lebensweg eines Baustoffs über die Stadien der Rohstoffgewinnung, Herstellung, Verarbeitung; gegebenenfalls werden auch Transport, Nutzung, Nachnutzung und Entsorgung berücksichtigt. Ihre Bilanzgrenze bestimmt maßgeblich, welche Informationen über den Ressourcenverbrauch und die Umweltauswirkungen gewonnen werden können.

LEED, Leadership in Energy and Environmental Design
LEED ist ein vom U.S. Green Building Council seit 1998 entwickeltes Klassifizierungssystem für die energie- und umweltfreundliche Planung von Gebäuden. Das international anerkannte Label definiert eine Reihe von Standards und wird in verschiedenen Kategorien, zum Beispiel für Bestandsgebäude, vergeben. Die ökologische Nachhaltigkeit wird aktuell in vier Qualitätsstufen eingeordnet: Certified (40–49 Punkte), Silver (50–59), Gold (60–79), Platinum (80 und mehr Punkte). Dies gilt für alle LEED-Zertifizierungen mit Ausnahme der für Wohngebäude (LEED for Homes).

Ökobilanz
Sie wird in der DIN EN ISO 14040 und DIN EN ISO 14044 definiert. Auf Basis der Materialaufwendungen rechnet sie Herstellung und Produktionsprozesse eines Produkts in seine Umweltverträglichkeit und Auswirkungen (zum Beispiel Emissionen) um. Die Methodik ist auch für die Untersuchung von Prozessen, Verfahren und Unternehmen anwendbar.

Passivhaus/zertifiziertes Passivhaus
Ein Gebäude mit einem bestimmten Energiestandard, bei dem unter anderem der Primärenergiebedarf maximal 120 kWh/m²a inklusive aller elektrischen Verbraucher betragen darf. Ein Passivhaus ist sehr gut wärmegedämmt und benötigt deshalb keine Heizungsanlage im herkömmlichen Sinn. Der Heizenergiebedarf wird überwiegend aus ‚passiven' Wärmegewinnen durch Sonneneinstrahlung und die Abwärme von Personen und technischen Geräten gedeckt, der verbleibende Bedarf durch eine kontrollierte Wohnraumlüftung mit Wärmerückgewinnung. Zur Qualitätssicherung bietet das Passivhaus Institut ein Zertifikat für Gebäude und einzelne Baukomponenten an.

Photovoltaik (PV)
Teil der Solartechnik, der Strahlungsenergie des Sonnenlichts unter Ausnutzung des Photoeffekts direkt in elektrische Energie umwandelt. Dies geschieht über zumeist aus Silizium hergestellte Solarzellen, die auf Bauwerken oder Freiflächen installiert sind.

Sole
Salz-Wasser-Lösung, die als Wärmeträger zum Beispiel in Wärmepumpen und Erdsonden für die Nutzung von Geothermie zum Einsatz kommt.

Wärmepumpe
Unter Zufuhr von technischer Arbeit (Strom) transportiert eine Wärmepumpe Wärme von einem niedrigeren zu einem höheren Temperaturniveau. In der Gebäudetechnik wird damit aus Luft, Wasser und Erdreich Energie gewonnen.

Wärmerückgewinnung (WRG)
Sammelbegriff für Verfahren, die thermische Energie innerhalb eines Systems wieder nutzbar machen und dadurch den Primärenergieverbrauch reduzieren. So werden auch Treibhausgase und CO_2-Emissionen vermieden. Die WRG hat die Aufgabe, die Potentiale von Energieströmen, die sonst in die Umwelt entlassen würden, zu nutzen. Ihr kommt somit die Eigenschaft einer erneuerbaren Energie zu.

Glossary

Heat pump
Through the supply of electrical energy (electricity), a heat pump transports heat from a lower temperature to a higher level. Hereby, in building technology, energy is gained out of the air, water and ground soil.

Heat recovery
General term for a process which makes thermal energy within a system reusable and thus reduces the primary energy consumption. Using this principle, global warming gases and CO_2 emissions are avoided. It has the task to reuse the potential of energy flows that would otherwise be transferred into the environment and lost. Thus, the recovered energy is assigned being renewable.

LEED, Leadership in Energy and Environmental Design
Since 1998 LEED is a classification system for energy and environmentally friendly design of buildings, developed by the U.S. Green Building Council. The internationally approved label defines a set of standards and is awarded in various categories, e.g. for existing buildings. Environmental sustainability is currently classified in four quality levels: Certified (40-49 points), Silver (50–59), Gold (60–79) and Platinum (80 + points). This applies to all LEED certificates except residential buildings (LEED for Homes).

Life cycle analysis (LCA)
The LCA takes into account the life cycle of a material through its recovery, production, processing, where applicable its transportation, usage, recycling and disposal. The audit parameters determine what information can be obtained through the consumption of resources and the environmental impact.

Passive House/certified Passive House
A building with a certain energy standard, in which, amongst others, the primary energy requirements, including all electrical needs, should not exceed 120 kWh/m^2a. A Passive House is well thermally insulated and does not need a heating system in the conventional sense. The heating demand is predominantly covered passively, through heat gained by sun rays and the waste heat from humans and technical equipment; the remaining energy demand is covered through a controlled ventilation system with heat recovery. For quality assurance, the Passive House Institute offers a certificate for buildings and individual building components.

Photovoltaic (PV)
Part of the solar energy technology, which transforms radiation energy of the sunlight directly into electrical energy by using the photoelectric effect. This is mostly done through solar cells made of silicium, which are installed on buildings or open spaces.

Renewable energies
Regenerative or alternative energy sources can be renewed relatively quickly or are inexhaustible, according to human judgement. These include solar radiation, geothermal, wind and water power as well as biomass/renewable resources.

Unterstützer und Sponsoren

 Handwerkskammer Frankfurt-Rhein-Main

Handwerkskammer Frankfurt-Rhein-Main
Bockenheimer Landstraße 21
D-60325 Frankfurt am Main
Telefon: 069-97 17 20
Telefax: 069-97 17 21 99
E-Mail: info@hwk-rhein-main.de
Web: www.hwk-rhein-main.de

Mainova AG
Solmsstraße 38
D-60623 Frankfurt am Main
Telefon: 0800-11 44 488
Telefax: 0800-11 55 588
E-Mail: info@mainova.de
Web: www.mainova.de

 messe frankfurt

Messe Frankfurt GmbH
Ludwig-Erhard-Anlage 1
D-60327 Frankfurt am Main
Telefon: 069-75 750
Telefax: 069-75 75 64 33
E-Mail: info@messefrankfurt.com
Web: www.messefrankfurt.com

In Zeiten globaler Ressourcenverknappung ist das Thema Nachhaltigkeit von größter Bedeutung – insbesondere für die Immobilienbranche. Die OFB Projektentwicklung übernimmt mit nachhaltigem Planen und Bauen Verantwortung für Umwelt und Gesellschaft.

Als Tochterunternehmen der Landesbank Hessen-Thüringen entwickelt die OFB seit über 50 Jahren erfolgreich Immobilien.

OFB Projektentwicklung GmbH
Speicherstraße 55 · 60327 Frankfurt am Main
Tel. +49 69 91732-01 · ofb-frankfurt@ofb.de
www.ofb.de

Helaba Immobiliengruppe

OFB
Projektentwicklung

SUBSTANZ SCHAFFT WERTE

Der BDB ist der mitgliederstärkste Verband von Bauschaffenden (Architekten aller Fachrichtungen und im Bauwesen tätige Ingenieure) in Deutschland.

In ihm sind Freiberufler, Angestellte, Beamte, Unternehmer und Studenten organisiert. Diese Struktur garantiert eine schlagkräftige Gemeinschaft.

Mit 20.000 Mitgliedern ist er ein wirkungsvolles Forum zur Förderung partnerschaftlicher Zusammenarbeit.

Der BDB verbessert die Chancen einer auf die menschlichen Bedürfnisse zugeschnittenen Umwelt, da er Bauen als ganzheitliche Aufgabe begreift.

www.bdb-frankfurt.de

BUND DEUTSCHER BAUMEISTER
ARCHITEKTEN UND INGENIEURE
FRANKFURT RHEIN MAIN E.V.

BAUEN
PLANEN KOORDINIEREN

ARCHITEKT BDB

INGENIEUR BDB

UNTERNEHMER BDB

WIR schaffen WERTE

Energie von morgen.
Für Sie schon heute.

Mit Erneuerbarer Energie versorgen wir die Region bereits heute: zum Beispiel mit Windkraft aus Siegbach und Hohenahr in Mittelhessen. Und wir investieren weiter in die nachhaltige Gegenwart – unter Einbeziehung der Menschen vor Ort, in Kooperation mit den Kommunen und im Einklang mit der Natur. **Mehr Erneuerbares: www.mainova.de**

BEWUSST LEBEN.

VERO erfüllt unter dem Aspekt der ökologischen Nachhaltigkeit höchste Ansprüche:

- Flexible Grundrissanpassung an wechselnde Lebensabschnitte
- Energieversorgung über Luft-Wasser Wärmepumpe
- Energieversorgung zur Spitzenlastabdeckung über Gas
- Sonnenkollektoren auf den Dächern zur Warmwassererzeugung
- Effiziente Wärmedämmung durch Wärmeverbundsystem und 3-fach-Verglasung
- DGNB-Siegel in Gold für nachhaltige Gebäudeplanung

+49 69/6 80 99-6 23
www.vero-westend.de

VERO — raum für das wesentliche. frankfurt westend.

DGNB

PATRIZIA
WERTE ENTSCHEIDEN

LEBENS-
WERTE
STADT
A CITY
FULL
OF LIFE

A project by

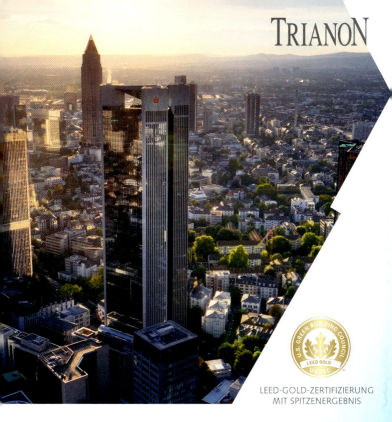

LEED-GOLD-ZERTIFIZIERUNG
MIT SPITZENERGEBNIS

Green Building auf höchstem Niveau

TRIANON
auf einen Blick

+ Erstklassige Büros mitten im Bankenviertel
+ Mainzer Landstraße 16, Frankfurt am Main
+ Höhe 186 m
+ 47 Obergeschosse
+ Mietfläche ca. 66.000 m²

TRIANON
auf einen Klick

www.trianon-frankfurt.de

Vermietung
Bilfinger Real Estate Argoneo GmbH 60322 Frankfurt am Main Tel. +49 69 244334-0

Photovoltaik und Energieeffizienz

Das Investment in eine Photovoltaik-(PV-)Anlage und deren wirtschaftlicher Betrieb setzen die gründliche Untersuchung einer Reihe von Erfolgsfaktoren voraus.
Unsere Experten verfügen über langjährige Erfahrung in der Beurteilung technischer Anlagen jeglicher Art und unterstützen Sie als Betreiber mit der Zertifizierung Ihrer PV-Anlagen gern.

Unser Leistungsportfolio umfasst außerdem:

- Energetische Bewertung von Gebäuden und Anlagen nach EnEV
- Konzepte zur Energieeinsparung
- Energetische Inspektion von Lüftungs- und Klimaanlagen nach §12 EnEV
- Thermografie Gutachten

TÜV Technische Überwachung Hessen GmbH
Bereich Industrie
Anlagentechnik-Renewables

Rüdesheimer Str. 119 ● 64285 Darmstadt
Telefon: 0800 8834377
info@tuevhessen.de

TÜV ®

www.tuev-hessen.de

HERZLICHEN GLÜCKWUNSCH!
MESSETURM FRANKFURT
LEED SILBER ZERTIFIZIERT

FRANKFURT IST UM EIN GREEN BUILDING REICHER!

WWW.MESSETURM.COM

Foto: Michael Wicander, www.skyline-frankfurt.com
Design: MoellerFeuerstein GmbH

EINE IMMOBILIE DER GLL REAL ESTATE PARTNERS GMBH

www.riedberg.

HA Stadtentwicklung
HA Stadtentwicklungsgesellschaft mbH

STADT FRANKFURT AM M.

ww.wisag.de

Gebäudetechnik

Energieeffizienz und ökologische Verantwortung. Unser Auftrag! Unser Leitbild!

Als Prozessdienstleister ist unser Anspruch, in unseren Märkten Vorbild für den Schutz unserer Umwelt zu sein. Wir helfen Ihnen, Verbräuche und Emissionen zu senken und die Energieeffizienz Ihrer Immobilie zu steigern. Wir gehen für Sie den einen Schritt weiter.

WISAG Gebäudetechnik Hessen GmbH & Co. KG
Rebstöcker Str. 35
D-60326 Frankfurt am Main

WISAG heißt Wertschätzung!
WISAG heißt Einsatz!
WISAG heißt bunt!

Entdecken Sie die schönsten Seiten der Stadt...

IM BRIEFKASTEN ... mit dem JOURNAL FRANKFURT

Das 14-tägige Stadtmagazin für Frankfurt & Rhein-Main mit einem umfangreichen Magazinteil, interessanten Stadtgeschichten, einem einzigartigen Kulturteil und:

- Tipps & Terminen für die Rubriken Musik, Party, Literatur, Kunst, Theater, Kinder und Gastro
- exklusiven Interviews
- großem Veranstaltungskalender
- TV-Programm
- Verlosungen, Gewinnspielen & Extras

JOURNAL FRANKFURT – alle 14 Tage für nur 1,80 € am Kiosk oder direkt im Abo unter:

www.journal-frankfurt.de/abo

PER E-MAIL ... mit JOURNAL · DER TAG

Das kostenlose eMAG (Mo–Fr) mit brandaktuellen Infos von Frankfurt & Rhein-Main für Ihren Tag:

- Nachrichten des Tages
- Veranstaltungen
- Kunst, Kultur, Gastronomie-Tipps

Jetzt kostenlos anmelden unter:

www.journal-der-tag.de

HAUTNAH ... mit den Frankfurter Stadtevents

Die Stadtführungen, Workshops & Fun-Pakete der anderen Art zu über 180 spannenden Themen wie zum Beispiel:

- Frankfurts „grüne" Architektur & Passivhäuser
- Kuriose Stadtgeschichten
- Lagenwanderungen
- Wildkräuter-Seminare
- Tatort Frankfurt
- Kulinarisches Ffm
- Weintouren
- „Grüne" Hochhäuser
- Führungen für Kinder

Alle Themen, Termine, Infos & Buchung unter:

www.frankfurter-stadtevents.de

Staatliche Vogelschutzwarte für Hessen, Rheinland-Pfalz und Saarland

Die Staatliche Vogelschutzwarte kümmert sich seit über 75 Jahren um den Vogelschutz in ihrem Geschäftsbereich. Sie

- berät die Länder Hessen, Rheinland-Pfalz und Saarland und die Stadt Frankfurt in ornithologischen Fachfragen
- betreut anwendungsorientierte Untersuchungen zur Ökologie und Biologie der Vögel
- beobachtet und bewertet die Bestandssituation wildlebender Vogelarten im Geschäftsbereich
- entwickelt, betreut und koordiniert Erfassungs- und Schutzprogramme für im Geschäftsbereich gefährdete Vogelarten
- bildet fort, insbesondere das Ehrenamt und die Fachverwaltungen
- betreibt selbständig Öffentlichkeitsarbeit in allgemeinen Fragen des Vogelschutzes

Gerne laden wir Sie zu unseren Veranstaltungen ein oder beantworten Ihre Fragen zum Vogelschutz. Aktuelles über unsere Arbeit und Veranstaltungen finden Sie auf unserer Homepage www.vswffm.de. Auch können Sie mit uns über info@vswffm.de in Kontakt treten.

Fütternder Star, Foto Alfred Limbrunner, Archiv VSW

Staatliche Vogelschutzwarte für Hessen, Rheinland-Pfalz und Saarland
Steinauer Straße 44, 60386 Frankfurt

Fotoverzeichnis, Karten und Pläne

Titelbild: Messe Frankfurt GmbH/Sutera

Übersichtskarte Umschlag vorne:
Geobasisdaten: © Stadtvermessungsamt Frankfurt am Main, Stand 01.2012, Lizenznummer 6233-7812-D/Bearbeitung: Smart Skript

Grußwort: Energiereferat der Stadt Frankfurt am Main

Service: Tourismus+Congress GmbH Frankfurt am Main, Fotograf Holger Ullmann

Netzplan Umschlag hinten: traffiQ Lokale Nahverkehrsgesellschaft Frankfurt am Main mbH

Karten der Routen:
Geobasisdaten: © Stadtvermessungsamt Frankfurt am Main, Stand 01.2012, Lizenznummer 6233-7812-D/Bearbeitung: Smart Skript

1 | Route Gallus
Seite 15: Smart Skript
Seite 16: ABG FRANKFURT HOLDING GmbH
Seite 17: Smart Skript
Seite 19, 20: OFB Projektentwicklung GmbH

2 | Route Sachsenhausen – Mainufer – Westhafen
Seite 22: Drexler Guinand Jauslin Architekten GmbH
Seite 25: Smart Skript
Seite 26: Museum Angewandte Kunst Frankfurt
Seite 27: Smart Skript
Seite 28: Städel Museum, Norbert Miguletz
Seite 30, 31: Smart Skript
Seite 32, 33: OFB Projektentwicklung GmbH
Seite 35, 36: Mainova
Seite 37: Smart Skript

3 | Route Westend Süd – Europaviertel – Westend Nord
Seite 40 oben: Olaf Dziallas Photographie, Frankfurt am Main
Seite 40 unten: Chris Kister, Frankfurt am Main
Seite 42, 43: Thomas Eicken
Seite 44, 47, 48, 49: CA Immo Deutschland GmbH
Seite 50: Michael Wicander
Seite 51: GLL Real Estate Partners GmbH
Seite 52: Messe Frankfurt GmbH
Seite 55: Smart Skript
Seite 57 links: Herwarth + Holz, Planung und Architektur, Berlin
Seite 57 rechts: K9 ARCHITEKTEN, Borgards.Lösch.Piribauer, Freiburg
Seite 58: KfW-Bildarchiv, Thomas Klewar
Seite 60: KfW-Bildarchiv
Seite 61: KfW-Bildarchiv, Thomas Klewar
Seite 64: Smart Skript

4 | Route Westend Süd – Innenstadt – Nordend
Seite 66, 67: PATRIZIA
Seite 70, 71: Thomas Eicken
Seite 72, 73: Alte Oper Frankfurt
Seite 75, 76: Smart Skript

Quellenverzeichnis

Seite 78: B & V Braun Canton Volleth Architekten GmbH, Fotografie Thomas Ott
Seite 79: B & V Braun Canton Volleth Architekten GmbH, Manfred Rohloff
Seite 81 links: ROOK architekten, Michael Bender
Seite 81 rechts: ROOK architekten, Anastasia Hermann, Berlin
Seite 82: Smart Skript

5 | Route City – Innenstadt und Altstadt

Seite 86, 87: OFB Projektentwicklung GmbH
Seite 88, 89: Landesbank Hessen-Thüringen (Helaba)
Seite 91 links: Gabriele Röhle, Commerzbank AG
Seite 91 rechts: Julia Schwager, Commerzbank AG
Seite 94: Helvetia Versicherungen, DailyArt-Frankfurt
Seite 95, 98, 99, 101: Smart Skript
Seite 102: Caritasverband Frankfurt e.V., Christian Eblenkamp

6 | Exkursionen

Seite 104, 105: Deutsche Börse AG
Seite 106, 107: Smart Skript
Seite 108, 109: Mainova
Seite 110, 111: Juri Troy
Seite 112: Cantón Thielen Architekten
Seite 113: Leclaire Photographie
Seite 115: ABG FRANKFURT HOLDING GmbH
Seite 116, 119: Smart Skript
Seite 121, 122: Eibe Sönnecken, Darmstadt
Seite 124, 125: Mainova
Seite 126: ABG FRANKFURT HOLDING GmbH, Jo. Franzke Architekten
Seite 127: ABG FRANKFURT HOLDING GmbH, Albert Speer & Partner GmbH
Seite 128: ABG FRANKFURT HOLDING GmbH, Jo. Franzke Architekten
Seite 129: HA Stadtentwicklungsgesellschaft mbH
Seite 131: HA Stadtentwicklungsgesellschaft mbH, Dirk Laubner, Berlin
Seite 132: Smart Skript
Seite 133: HA Stadtentwicklungsgesellschaft mbH

Quellen

| Frankfurter ArchitekTour. Buch. B3 Verlag Frankfurt am Main.2009.
| Green Building Award 2011. Broschüre. Hrsg. von der Stadt Frankfurt am Main, Energiereferat.2012.
| Klimasparbuch Frankfurt 2012. Buch. Hrsg. von der Stadt Frankfurt am Main, Energiereferat, und oekom e.V. – Verein für ökologische Kommunikation.2011.
| Nachhaltige Gebäude Frankfurt Rhein-Main. pdf-Datei. Hrsg. von der Stadt Frankfurt am Main, Energiereferat, und AiD Architektur im Dialog. Erstellt im Dezember 2011.

| Informationen, die die im Buch genannten Organisationen sowie die Stadt Frankfurt am Main der Redaktion zur Verfügung stellten.

| Internetauftritte der im Buch genannten Institutionen, Architekten, Bauten sowie der Stadt Frankfurt am Main
| www.frankfurt-tourismus.de
| www.juedisches-frankfurt.de
| www.wikipedia.de

Alle Angaben und Informationen sind gewissenhaft zusammengetragen und überprüft worden. Dennoch sind Fehler nicht immer vollständig zu vermeiden.

Der Weststadt Verlag, das Energiereferat der Stadt Frankfurt am Main und Smart Skript sind bestrebt, in allen Publikationen die Urheberrechte der verwendeten Fotos und Texte zu beachten. Die Herausgeber übernehmen keinerlei Gewähr für Korrektheit und Vollständigkeit der bereitgestellten Informationen. Soweit nicht anders angegeben, liegen die Rechte der Abbildungen und Texte bei den Urhebern.

Index

Energieeffizienz-Projekte/
Energy-efficient buildings

Alte Oper	72/73
Baseler Arkaden	36/37
Biomasse-Kraftwerk Fechenheim	124/123
Blockheizkraftwerk Palmengarten	64/65
Bonifatiusschule	54/55
Campo am Bornheimer Depot	114/115
Caritas Quartier	100/101
City Haus I, DZ-Bank	42/43
Commerzbank-Hochhaus	90/91
Deutsche Börse	104/105
Dom-Römer-Areal	96/99
Europaviertel	46/47
Frankensteiner Hof	24/25
Gebäude Max-Hirsch-Straße	118/117
Gelände der ehemaligen Bremsenfabrik von Alfred Teves	20/21
Geschosswohnungen Tevesstraße	16/17
Graues Haus	112/113
Gymnasium Riedberg	128/129
Heinrich-Lübke-Siedlung	126/125
Heizkraftwerk West	34/33
Helvetia Bürogebäude	94/95
Junghof	84/87
Kap Europa	46/47
KfW Haupthaus	60/63
KfW Ostarkade	60/61
KfW Westarkade	58/59
Kulturcampus	56/57
Ludwig-Börne-Schule	82/83
Main Building	70/71
Main Tower	88/89
Maintor Quartier	102/103
Mehrfamilienhaus Ackermannstraße	14/15
Messehalle 10	52/53
Messeturm	50/51
Michael-Grzimek-Schule	110/111
Minimum Impact House	22/23
Müllheizkraftwerk Nordweststadt	108/109
Museum Angewandte Kunst	26/27
Nextower	76/77
Ökohaus Arche	106/107
Opernturm	70/71
Ordnungsamt	18/19
Projekt Vero	66/67
Scheffelhof	78/79
Skyline Plaza	46/47
Staatliche Vogelschutzwarte	120/121
Städel Museum	28/29
Stadtteil Riedberg	128/129
Stiftung Waisenhaus	78/79
Tower 185	44/45
Trianon	38/41
Türme der Deutschen Bank	38/39
Westend Gate	54/55
Westhafenkontor/Straßenverkehrsamt	30/31
Westhafen Tower	28/29
Wohnblocks Rotlintstraße	118/117

Abkürzungsverzeichnis/
List of abbreviations

CO_2 = Kohlendioxid/Carbon dioxide

EnEV = Energieeinsparverordnung/Energy saving guideline

GW = Gigawatt

ha = Hektar/Hectare

km = Kilometer

kW = Kilowatt

kWh = Kilowattstunde/Kilowatt hour

kWh/(m²a) = Kilowattstunde pro Quadratmeter und Jahr/Kilowatt hour per square meter and year

kWh/m² = Kilowattstunde pro Quadratmeter/Kilowatt hour per square meter

m² = Quadratmeter/Square meter

mg/m³ = Milligramm pro Kubikmeter/Milligramme per cubic meter

MW = Megawatt

t = Tonne/Metric ton

W = Watt